A SEASON
of
CELEBRATING

The Museum of Science and Industry, Chicago
Copyright© 1997 The Museum of Science and Industry, Chicago
57th Street and Lake Shore Drive
Chicago, Illinois 60637
1-773-684-1414

Library of Congress Catalog Number: 97-75240
ISBN: 0-9638657-6-5

For The Museum of Science and Industry, Chicago:
President and CEO: Dr. James S. Kahn
Director of Business Administration: Nancy L. Wright
Manager of Product Development: Jennifer J. Wood

Project Coordinator and Writer: Erin Okamato Protsman

Designed, edited, and manufactured by
Favorite Recipes® Press
an imprint of

FRP™

P.O. Box 305142
Nashville, TN 37230
1-800-358-0560

Art Director: Steve Newman
Recipe Editor: Christie St. John, PhD
Project Manager: Elizabeth Miller, JD
Book Designer: Mark Föltz

Cover Photography: Courtesy of Hedrich Blessing
All Architectural Photography: Courtesy of Anthony Arciero

Manufactured in the United States of America
First Printing: 1997   10,000 copies

CONTENTS

ACKNOWLEDGEMENTS

—◈—

The Museum of Science and Industry wishes to express its grateful appreciation to the following organizations that have generously contributed to the making of this cookbook.

Armenian Youth Federation
Belarusian American National Council
    of Chicago
Belizean Cultural Association
Bielarusian Coordinating Committee of Chicago
Calvin Reformed Church of Lynwood, Illinois
Cambrian Benevolent Society of Chicago
The Canadian Women's Club of Chicago
Centenary United Methodist Church of
    Los Angeles
Chicago Board of Rabbis
Chicago Ecuadorean Lions Club
Chicago Mexica Lions Club
Chicago Museum Committee
Chinese American Civic Council
Club Bedrich Smetana
Consulate General of Guatemala
Consulate General of Israel to the Midwest
Croatian Women's Organization, Branch 1,
    Chicago, Illinois
Danish American Athletic Club
Danish Sisterhood Society, Olga Lodge 11
Embassy of Israel
Federation of Circles of Serbian Sisters,
    Midwestern Metropolitanate of the Serbian
    Orthodox Church
Finnladies of Chicagoland

German-American Children's Chorus
India Catholic Association of America
Irish American Heritage Center
Joint Civic Committee of Italian Americans
Knights of Lithuanian Dancers
Lansing Business Women's Association
Linnea South Suburban Swedish
    Women's Club
Luxembourg News of America
Native American Tree Committee
Peiraikon Hellenic School
Polish Scouting Organization, Z.H.P.—Inc.
The Romanian Christmas Group Holy Nativity
Sacred Heart Croatian School, Kolo and
    Tambura Group
St. Mark's Coptic Church
Sampaguita Singers of Chicago, Inc.
Society of the Danube Swabians
Spertus Museum of Judaica
Stars of the South Pacific
Swiss Club of Chicago
Thistle & Heather Highland Dancers
Tampopo-Kai
Ukrainian National Women's League,
    Branch 22, in Chicago
Villa Scalabrini Home for the Aged

FOREWORD

—⁓—

Dear Friends,

In the early 1940s, The Museum of Science and Industry, with the cooperation of members of Chicago's ethnic communities, presented its first "Christmas Around the World" exhibit. The original event was designed to bring members of the community together and to share with our visitors the many ways in which Christmas is celebrated in various cultures. Over the years many people have generously donated their time, their handicrafts, and their tireless spirit to make this festival a Chicago tradition.

The exhibit was so successful that a second festival blossomed forth from the Christmas gala: the joyous, colorful "Holidays of Light," which debuted in 1994. This pagentry of holidays presents a wide range of cultural celebrations, such as Chinese New Year, Diwali, Hanukkah, Kwanzaa, Ramadan, Eid-Ul-Fitr, St. Lucia Day, and Visakha Puja Day.

What is remarkable about both these events is the continuing close-knit partnership between the Museum and the wonderful people from various ethnic affiliations and religions who participate. It is a shining example of Chicago at its best!

While one of the most interesting features is an observance of the diverse cultural heritage in this country, another is the sharing of a wealth of different foods. Food is an integral part of celebrating—and where else but at The Museum of Science and Industry could one find such a global festival of light, song, food, and family!

We received the recipes and stories in this book from members of our community, and it is with great pleasure that we share these treasures and customs with you.

Dr. James S. Kahn
President and CEO

INTRODUCTION

———

Experiencing the magic of The Museum of Science and Industry's "Christmas Around the World" festival has become an annual holiday tradition for hundreds of thousands of Chicago area families and friends. Who would have guessed that this simple celebration would grow to be such a popular Chicago custom, standing the test of time for well over five decades?

The Museum's first Christmas festival was created in 1942 by the late Major Lenox Lohr, the Museum's first president. The festival was Lohr's way of honoring Chicago's ethnic communities whose native countries were allied with the United States during World War II. During the festival's first year, one live Christmas tree was featured. With the help of volunteers recruited from various Chicago communities, this lone tree was decorated each evening by a different group for display the following morning. The Christmas tree stood in the Museum for only two weeks and featured handmade ornaments from around the world. Traditional ethnic holiday foods were served at lunch time and flags from twenty-nine nations were suspended from the balcony in the Museum's North Court.

Due to the popularity of this first effort, the ethnic communities were invited back to the Museum the following year. This time, each group decorated its own individual tree to resemble trees displayed in the homes of their native land. Theater pageants were also added to the festivities, treating visitors to songs, dances, and celebrations of different cultures. Although the display was first named "Christmas in the United Nations" and later "Around the World at Christmas," the celebration was dubbed "Christmas Around the World" in the late 1940s. As the decades passed, "Christmas Around the World" became increasingly popular with visitors, and the Museum enjoyed the support of more and more community organizations that wanted to share their holiday customs.

In 1994, the Museum's holiday festivities expanded further to include a new display called "Holidays of Light." This multicultural exhibition celebrates a variety of holidays that feature light or enlightenment as the central theme. Each year, eight holidays are highlighted in displays encased in a stunning flame sculpture.

Today, the "Christmas Around the World" and "Holidays of Light" festivals are supported by over sixty ethnic communities and organizations throughout the Chicago area. Visitors enjoy the sights and sounds of the holidays as they walk through a forest of more than forty beautifully decorated Christmas trees and creches, and they marvel at the displays in the equally striking "Holidays of Light" sculpture. Visitors are also treated to an extensive array of international pageants and programming designed to satisfy many different tastes.

Of course, food has always been an important part of holiday festivals, not only at The Museum of Science and Industry but in homes around the world. This cookbook is filled with tried and true family recipes from the people who make "Christmas Around the World" and "Holidays of Light" truly special. Many of these recipes have been passed down from generation to generation and are shared throughout the ethnic communities by friends and family members. Each recipe comes with its own special story or memory, many of which appear in this cookbook.

Sincere thanks are given to all the individuals and organizations who shared their recipes, holiday traditions, and special stories with us. We now have the opportunity to re-experience the dishes familiar to our own ethnic backgrounds, and to taste new and exotic flavors from around the world, representing the holidays of Christmas, Diwali, Hanukkah, Kwanzaa, Chinese New Year, St. Lucia Day, and Shogatsu.

Enjoy!

DEDICATION

—✦—

The Museum of Science and Industry developed *A Season of Celebrating*
as a lasting tribute to all of the community organizations, past and present,
that have participated in "Christmas Around the World" and
"Holidays of Light" over the years. These organizations' support for the Museum
and their rich cultural heritage show in the intricate ornaments they make,
the expressive songs they sing, the detailed displays they create,
the poignant stories they tell, and the delicious recipes they share.

CHAPTER One

BEVERAGES & APPETIZERS

A SEASON
of
CELEBRATING

Holiday Memories

❦

How exciting to know that billions of people around our world
celebrate an array of holidays in such diverse and wonderful ways.
Togetherness and sharing—especially of food—
highlight our experiences. Take a peek at just a few of the holidays
and traditions that have been passed down over a countless
number of generations, in homes near and far, that give us
the joyful memories of holidays past and make us anticipate
the holidays of our future.

Israel

MINT TEA

Mint leaves, which can be grown at home, are particularly favored as a cooling, refreshing addition to salads and beverages in the hot climate of Israel.

8	teaspoons sugar
4	tea bags
2	teaspoons fresh mint leaves
4	dashes lemon salt
5	cups boiling water

Place the sugar, tea bags, mint leaves and lemon salt in a teapot. Add the boiling water. Let steep until of desired taste.

Yield: 4 to 5 servings

Embassy of Israel and Consulate General of Israel to the Midwest

Israel

TURKISH COFFEE

1	tablespoon finely ground Turkish coffee
1	teaspoon (or more) sugar
	Cardamom pods to taste

Mix the coffee and the sugar in a feenjan or small saucepan. Add 1 serving cup of boiling water; stir well. Add cardamom pods. Bring the coffee to a boil. Remove from the heat when the foam starts to rise; let foam settle slightly. Repeat this process twice. Pour into a coffee cup, spooning in some of the foam. Do not stir, allowing coffee grounds to settle at the bottom of the cup. Serve immediately.

Yield: 1 serving

Embassy of Israel and Consulate General of Israel to the Midwest

BEVERAGES & APPETIZERS

DRINKING TURKISH COFFEE IS PART OF THE DAILY LIFE IN ISRAEL, AND IS THE MOST POPULAR BEVERAGE IN THE COUNTRY. THE COFFEE TASTES BEST WHEN PREPARED IN A FEENJAN, A POT THAT IS WIDE AT THE BOTTOM AND NARROW AT THE TOP AND HAS A LONG HANDLE. THESE ARE AVAILABLE AT MIDDLE EASTERN SPECIALTY SHOPS, AS IS THE TURKISH COFFEE. THE COFFEE CAN BE BREWED IN A SMALL, DEEP SAUCEPAN AND SHOULD BE SERVED IN SMALL STRAIGHT-SIDED CUPS, SUCH AS ESPRESSO CUPS.

In Lithuania, all family members make an effort to come home for the Christmas Eve supper . . . for this sacred family ritual draws the family closer, bonding everyone and strengthening warm family ties.

Lithuania
Poppy Seed Milk

1   (12-ounce) can poppy seed filling, or soaked, drained and ground poppy seeds, sweetened to taste
1   cup warm water
1   quart warm milk

Combine the poppy seed filling, water and milk in a large pitcher, stirring well. Let stand to cool. Serve in cups or pour over *Slizikai* (Christmas Eve Biscuits, page 128).

Yield: 6 to 8 servings

Lydia Ringus, Knights of Lithuanian Dancers

Sik Hae *Korea*
Rice Punch

3   cups yut ki loom powder (malted barley powder)
5   quarts warm water
2   cups rice
1   ounce gingerroot, sliced
1½ cups sugar
2   teaspoons pine nuts

Soak the yut ki loom powder in warm water for 2 to 3 hours or until the liquid turns a milky color. Strain the liquid through a paper towel-lined strainer into a large saucepan; set aside. Rinse the rice in cold water. Soak in water for 30 minutes. Place in a steamer. Steam for 30 minutes or until tender. Add to the strained liquid. Place in a warm oven (147 degrees to 166 degrees) for 2 to 3 hours or until the rice floats to the top. Skim off the rice. Rinse with cold water and set aside. Bring the strained liquid to a boil over medium heat. Add the gingerroot and sugar. Bring to a second boil; reduce the heat to low. Simmer for 10 minutes. Remove and discard the gingerroot. Let the liquid stand to cool. Chill in the refrigerator. Add the rice and pine nuts before serving.

Yield: 32 servings

Alycia Wright and Alice Jung

BISHOP'S WINE

1	orange
15	whole cloves
1	stick of cinnamon
1/2	apple
1/2	cup sugar
2	bottles claret (red bordeaux wine)
	Apple juice (optional)

Stud the orange evenly with the cloves. Combine with the cinnamon, apple, sugar and wine in a large saucepan. Simmer over very low heat for 30 minutes; do not boil. May stir in apple juice to lighten the wine. Remove the fruit and cinnamon before serving. Ladle into heatproof cups.

Yield: 16 servings

Margie Rysner, Chicago Museum Committee

RAISIN PUNCH

1	pound golden raisins
1 1/4	cups sugar
1	cup water
1	stick of cinnamon
3 1/2	cups sweet white wine
1/2	cup vodka

Rinse the raisins in hot water; drain. Combine the sugar and water in a heavy saucepan. Simmer until the sugar is dissolved. Add the cinnamon and raisins. Simmer over low heat until the raisins are plumped. Remove the raisins with a slotted spoon and place in an airtight glass container or bottle. Bring the liquid to a boil. Cook for 5 to 6 minutes or until slightly thickened. Pour over the raisins. Cool thoroughly. Pour in the wine and the vodka. Seal the bottle. Let stand for 1 to 2 months before serving. Serve in tall wine glasses with small demitasse spoons to eat the raisins.

Yield: 16 servings

Henny Bos, Chicago Museum Committee

BEVERAGES & APPETIZERS

CHRISTMAS GIFTS ARE GIVEN TO CELEBRATE ST. NICHOLAS DAY ON DECEMBER 5 IN THE NETHERLANDS. AT THE END OF AN EXCITING DAY OF SURPRISES, FAMILIES BEGIN TO RELAX. THE CHILDREN ENJOY SWEETS AND HOT CHOCOLATE BEFORE GOING TO BED, WHILE THE ADULTS HAVE PASTRIES AND COFFEE, OR STEAMY BISSCHOPSWIJN, A DELICIOUS HOT SPICED WINE THAT TOPS OFF THE EVENING PERFECTLY.

A FAVORITE HOLIDAY PUNCH IN THE NETHERLANDS, RAISIN PUNCH IS SERVED AT CHRISTMAS AND NEW YEAR'S EVE. IT IS BEST WHEN MADE WELL IN ADVANCE OF THE HOLIDAYS (AT LEAST ONE MONTH) TO ALLOW IT TIME TO MELLOW.

Sweden
SWEDISH GLÖGG

This is always served at Christmas parties.

1 gallon dry red wine

2 cups water

1/2 cup bourbon

1 cup 100 proof vodka

3 dashes angostura bitters

1 1/2 cups sugar

Peel of 1 orange

8 prunes

1 ounce ground cloves

2 to 3 sticks of cinnamon

1 teaspoon ground cardamom

1/2 cup blanched almonds

2 cups raisins

Combine the wine, water, bourbon, vodka, bitters and sugar in a large saucepan. Tie the orange peel, prunes, cloves, cinnamon and cardamom in a cheesecloth bag. Place in the saucepan. Heat over medium heat until the liquid begins to simmer; reduce the heat to low. Simmer, covered, for 1 hour. Add almonds and raisins. Simmer for 30 minutes longer. Serve warm.

Yield: 16 servings

Gail Bergren, Lansing Business Women's Association

Mexico
TEQUILA COCKTAIL

2 shot glasses of tequila

1/2 ounce grenadine syrup

Juice of 1 lime

Crushed ice

Combine the tequila, grenadine, lime juice and ice in a cocktail shaker. Shake well. Pour into chilled glasses. May salt rims of glasses.

Yield: 1 to 2 servings

Theresa Ochoa, Chicago Mexica Lions Club

Baba Ghanouj *Israel*
EGGPLANT WITH TAHINI

1 large eggplant

1 medium onion

¹/₂ bunch parsley, finely chopped

¹/₂ cup tahini

2 tablespoons lemon juice

2 cloves of garlic, crushed

2 teaspoons water

1 teaspoon salt

Dash of cayenne pepper

Bake the whole eggplant in a pan at 450 degrees for 30 minutes or until the skin is charred and the eggplant is tender, or place directly on a gas burner over a medium flame, turning as the skin blackens and the eggplant becomes tender. Let cool slightly. Slice into halves lengthwise. Scoop out the pulp with a wooden spoon to preserve the flavor. Chop finely in a ceramic or wooden bowl. Grate the onion coarsely, squeezing out the juice. Mix the onion and parsley with the eggplant. Blend the tahini with the lemon juice and garlic, adding water gradually until the mixture turns white. Stir into the eggplant mixture. Season with salt and cayenne pepper. May add additional lemon juice. Garnish with parsley and serve with pita bread triangles or crackers.

Yield: 2¹/₂ to 3 cups

Embassy of Israel and Consulate General of Israel to the Midwest

Hummus *Lebanon*
CHICK-PEA AND TAHINI PURÉE

1 (16-ounce) can chick-peas (garbanzo beans)

6 tablespoons tahini

3 cloves of garlic, mashed

Juice of 2 lemons

1 to 2 tablespoons olive oil

Drain the chick-peas, reserving 2 tablespoons of the liquid. Process the chick-peas, the reserved liquid, tahini, garlic and the juice of 1 lemon in a blender container until puréed and thick. Add enough of the remaining lemon juice for desired taste and consistency. Spread in a shallow serving bowl. Pour a small amount of olive oil in the center. Garnish with chopped parsley and sprinkle with paprika or cayenne pepper. Serve with pita bread.

Yield: 4 to 6 servings

Anita Kropp

Romania
CHEESE-STUFFED EGGS

8 hard-cooked eggs

2 egg yolks

1 tablespoon sour cream

3 tablespoons feta cheese

2 teaspoons finely
chopped dillweed

Salt and pepper to taste

¼ cup shredded
mozzarella cheese

Shell the eggs and slice into halves lengthwise. Remove the cooked yolks to a bowl. Add the raw egg yolks, sour cream, feta cheese, dillweed, salt and pepper; mix well. Spoon into the cooked egg whites. Place in a baking dish. Sprinkle with the mozzarella cheese. Bake at 400 degrees for 15 minutes or until golden brown. Arrange on lettuce leaves on a serving plate. Garnish with colorful sliced vegetables.

Yield: 16 servings

*Doina Dadurian, The Romanian Christmas Group
Holy Nativity*

Romania
TURKEY IN ASPIC

2 pig's feet

2½ quarts water

2 teaspoons salt

2 turkey wings

1 turkey leg

8 ounces turkey breast

4 cloves of garlic,
crushed

Boil the pig's feet in water to cover in a saucepan for 2 minutes. Drain and rinse well. Place in a 4-quart stockpot with 2½ quarts water and salt. Simmer over very low heat for 2 hours. Add the turkey pieces, 1 at a time. Simmer for 4 to 5 hours longer or until the liquid is reduced by one half. Remove the turkey with a slotted spoon and arrange in a glass serving bowl. Stir the garlic into the cooking liquid. Strain the liquid, discarding the garlic and pig's feet; pour over the turkey. Let cool. Chill, covered with plastic wrap, in the refrigerator for 4 to 5 hours or until congealed. Serve with mustard, lemon juice or vinegar on the side.

Yield: 6 to 8 servings

*Doina Dadurian, The Romanian Christmas Group
Holy Nativity*

Canada
BACON-CHEESE STRIP APPETIZERS

8   slices bacon, crisp-
     fried, crumbled

1   small onion, grated

8   ounces sharp Cheddar
     cheese, grated

1   cup mayonnaise

2   teaspoons
     Worcestershire sauce

1/2   cup sliced almonds

16   slices bread

Mix the bacon, onion, cheese, mayonnaise, Worcestershire sauce and almonds in a small bowl. Spread over one side of the bread slices. Cut each piece of bread into 3 equal strips; place on a baking sheet. Let stand for 1 hour to dry. Place, covered, in the freezer until frozen. Bake, uncovered, at 400 degrees for 10 to 15 minutes or until bubbly.

Yield: 48 servings

The Canadian Women's Club of Chicago

CRETONS *Canada*
PORK PÂTÉ

This appetizer recipe is similar to that served at L'Âtre, Ile d'Orléans, Québec.

3   pounds ground pork

3   cups dry bread crumbs

1   onion, minced

1   teaspoon ground cloves

3   cups milk

3   cloves of garlic,
     mashed, minced

    Salt and pepper to taste

Combine the ground pork, bread crumbs, onion, cloves, milk, garlic, salt and pepper in a heavy saucepan. Simmer, covered, over very low heat for 2 hours, stirring occasionally. Pack firmly into a meat loaf pan or a bowl. Place in the refrigerator until well chilled. Serve spread over French bread or crackers with mustard.

Yield: 24 to 36 servings

The Canadian Women's Club of Chicago

In Poland, the appearance
of the first star in the
sky was the signal for
the holiday festivities to
begin. The Wigilia
(Christmas Eve meal) is
traditionally meatless, and
in the past, there were
twelve main dishes.

SILKES SU POMIDORU PADAZU *Lithuania*
HERRING IN TOMATO SAUCE

2   whole herring
2   onions, sliced
      lengthwise
$^1/_2$ cup tomato paste
$^1/_4$ cup oil
$1^1/_2$ teaspoons white pepper
1   teaspoon sugar
$^1/_4$ cup white vinegar
1   tablespoon hot water

Place the herring in cold water in a glass bowl.
Let stand in a cool place for 48 hours, changing
the water every 12 hours. Clean and fillet,
discarding skin and bones. Cut into small
pieces. Place in a small glass serving dish.
Combine the onions, tomato paste, oil, pepper,
sugar, vinegar and water in a saucepan. Bring
to a boil; reduce the heat. Simmer until the
onions are tender. Cool completely. Pour over
the herring pieces, mixing well. Chill, covered,
in the refrigerator for 8 to 10 hours.

Yield: 6 to 8 servings

Lydia Ringus, Knights of Lithuanian Dancers

ŚLEDZIE MARYNOWANE W ŚMIETANIE *Poland*
PICKLED HERRING IN SOUR CREAM

6   pickled herring,
      drained
1   large onion, minced
6   hard-cooked eggs,
      chopped
1   apple, chopped
1   teaspoon lemon juice
1   cup sour cream
1   clove of garlic, crushed
      (optional)
$^1/_4$ teaspoon salt
$^1/_8$ teaspoon pepper
2   tablespoons freshly
      chopped dill or
      parsley

Cut the herring into small cubes. Combine
with the onion, eggs, apple and lemon juice in
a bowl. Mix the sour cream, garlic, salt and
pepper in a small bowl. Stir into the herring
mixture. Sprinkle with dill or parsley. Serve
with dark bread.

Yield: 4 to 6 servings

Polish Scouting Organization, Z.H.P.—Inc.

DANISH MEATBALLS

Frikadeller are served in all Danish homes. They can be used as an
appetizer at a buffet or for a main course at dinner.

1	pound ground pork
1	teaspoon salt
1/2	teaspoon pepper
1	medium onion, minced
2	eggs, beaten
3/4	cup milk
6	tablespoons flour
	Butter

Combine the ground pork, salt, pepper, onion and eggs in a mixer bowl. Beat at low speed until mixed. Add the milk gradually, beating at low speed. Stir in the flour. Chill, covered, for 30 minutes. Shape into 1-inch balls for appetizers, or make larger for main course servings. Fry in butter in a skillet for 5 minutes on each side or until browned and cooked through.

Yield: 32 small or 18 large meatballs

Yelva Baelum, Danish American Athletic Club

THERE ARE MANY VERSIONS OF SCANDINAVIAN MEATBALLS. THE PRINCIPAL DIFFERENCES ARE THE LIQUID USED (WATER, MILK OR CREAM) AND THE SPICES (NUTMEG, GINGER, ALLSPICE).

―――

KÖTTBULLAR IS A JUSTLY FAMOUS SWEDISH DISH AND IS ALWAYS FOUND ON THE SMÖRGÅSBORD. A CHOICE CUT OF BEEF SHOULD BE SELECTED AND GROUND AT HOME FOR BEST RESULTS. THE MIXTURE MAY BE USED FOR MEAT LOAF, MEAT PATTIES, ON SANDWICHES OR FOR MEATBALLS.

SMÅ KÖTTBULLAR *Sweden*
SWEDISH MEATBALLS

1/4	cup minced onion
1	tablespoon shortening
1/3	cup water
1/3	cup cream
1/4	cup fine, dry bread crumbs
3/4	pound ground round steak
1/4	pound lean ground pork
2	teaspoons salt
1/4	teaspoon pepper
	Dash of ground cloves
1/3	cup butter or margarine
1/4	cup boiling water

Sauté the onion in the shortening in a sauté pan until the onion is golden brown. Mix 1/3 cup water with the cream in a small bowl. Add the bread crumbs to soak. Combine with the onion, ground round, ground pork, salt, pepper and cloves in a large bowl; mix well. Shape into small balls, using 1 teaspoon of the mixture for each. Brown evenly in butter in a skillet, shaking the skillet to keep the meatballs round. Add the boiling water. Simmer, covered, for 5 to 10 minutes or until tender.

Yield: 70 small meatballs

Aina Momquist, Linnea South Suburban Swedish Women's Club

CHRISTMAS EVE IS THE MOST PIOUS EVE IN BELARUS. THE FOOD IS PREPARED AHEAD OF TIME AND IS SERVED AS SOON AS THE FIRST STAR APPEARS IN THE SKY.

———

GREEK APPETIZERS ARE AN ESSENTIAL PART OF GREEK LIFE AND ARE SERVED AS LIGHT MEALS BECAUSE DINNER IS SERVED LATE. THIS PAUSE ALLOWS ONE TO RELAX AND CONVERSE WITH FAMILY AND FRIENDS. THE APPETIZERS ARE ALWAYS ACCOMPANIED BY OUZO OR WINE.

SPINATNAJA ZAPIAKANKA *Belarus*
SPINACH SQUARES

1	(10-ounce) package frozen chopped spinach, thawed
2	eggs, beaten
1	teaspoon salt
1/2	cup melted butter
16	ounces Monterey Jack cheese, shredded
1	cup milk
1	cup flour
1	teaspoon baking powder

Drain the spinach, squeezing out excess moisture. Combine with the eggs, salt, butter, cheese, milk, flour and baking powder in a bowl; mix well. Spoon into a lightly greased baking dish. Cover with aluminum foil. Bake at 350 degrees for 40 to 45 minutes. Cool slightly and cut into squares to serve.

Yield: 15 servings

Anna Bruszkiewicz and Lucy Jalamov,
Bielarusian Coordinating Committee of Chicago

TIROPITA *Greece*
CHEESE PASTRIES

16	ounces feta cheese, crumbled
1 1/2	pounds ricotta cheese
2	to 3 tablespoons grated Kefalotiri cheese
4	egg yolks, beaten
	Dash of nutmeg and cinnamon
1	pound filo dough
1/2	cup melted butter

Combine the feta, ricotta and Kefalotiri cheeses in a bowl. Add the egg yolks, nutmeg and cinnamon; mix well. Cut the filo dough into 2 3/4-inch wide strips; brush with melted butter. Work with only a small amount of the dough at a time and keep the remaining dough covered to avoid drying. Spoon 1 teaspoon of the cheese mixture at one corner of the dough. Fold up to form a triangle; brush with butter. Repeat until the cheese mixture is used up. Place on a baking sheet. Bake at 350 degrees for 20 to 25 minutes or until golden brown. Serve hot.

Yield: 150 appetizers

Sophie Liambotis, Peiraikon Hellenic School

CHAPTER Two

SOUPS & SALADS

A SEASON
of
CELEBRATING

CHRISTMAS

———— ⟩⟩⟩ ————

In many European countries, special gestures and elaborate meals help break the monotony of a dark and wintery Christmas season. On Christmas Eve, families in Belarus, Poland, Ukraine, Lithuania, and Italy, serve a delicious, twelve course, meatless meal which symbolizes the twelve apostles. In German homes, a pickle is cleverly hidden in the Christmas tree for children to search for on Christmas morning. Trees decorated in Hungary are adorned with aromatic honey cakes. Across the world, Canadian children are apt to find their stockings stuffed to the brim with peppermint sticks and oranges, while in Mexico family members are treated to mouthwatering enchiladas, tortillas, sugar cookies and Mexican chocolate. In Guatemala, of course, it's not Christmas without tamales!

Avgolemono *Greece*
Egg Lemon Soup

6 cups strong chicken or lamb broth, strained

$^1/_4$ to $^1/_2$ cup rice

Salt to taste

1 egg

2 egg yolks

Juice of 2 lemons ($^1/_4$ cup)

Bring the chicken broth to a boil in a saucepan. Add the rice. Cook until tender. Season with salt. Beat the egg and egg yolks in a medium bowl. Add the lemon juice, beating well with a rotary beater. Pour in a small amount of the broth, beating constantly to avoid curdling. Pour this into the broth gradually, stirring constantly. Manestra or rosa marina may be substituted for rice.

Yield: 8 to 10 servings

Joanne Sideris, Peiraikon Hellenic School

Basler Mehlsuppe *Switzerland*
Flour Soup

10 tablespoons flour

$^1/_2$ cup butter

2 onions, chopped

8 cups clear beef broth

1 cup shredded Gruyère cheese

Heat a large skillet over low heat. Add the flour. Cook until golden brown; remove from the heat to cool. Melt the butter in a 2-quart saucepan. Add the cooled flour and mix well. Add the onions. Cook, covered, over very low heat for 3 to 5 minutes to steam the onions. Add the beef broth. Bring to a boil, stirring constantly; reduce the heat. Simmer for 20 minutes, stirring occasionally. Serve in warmed soup plates, topped with the cheese.

Yield: 8 servings

Beatrice Weiss, Swiss Club of Chicago

Soups & Salads

LEMON IS A PRIMARY INGREDIENT IN GREEK CUISINE AND IS USED TO FLAVOR THIS WELL-KNOWN GREEK SOUP, AVGOLEMONO. THIS SOUP IS SERVED BOTH DURING THE HOLIDAYS AND ON SUNDAYS.

———

THE BASLER MEHLSUPPE IS A SPECIALTY OF BASEL AND IS TRADITIONALLY SERVED DURING CARNIVAL TIME IN FEBRUARY. THE WELL-KNOWN BASEL CARNIVAL BEGINS WITH A LANTERN PARADE AT 4 A.M. ON THE MONDAY AFTER ASH WEDNESDAY. AFTER THE PARADE, PEOPLE GATHER IN THEIR FAVORITE RESTAURANTS TO WARM UP WITH THIS SPECIAL SOUP.

BUROKELIU SRIUBA SU AUSIKEMIS *Lithuania*

BEET SOUP WITH "LITTLE EARS"

1	carrot, sliced
1	rib of celery, sliced
1	onion, cut into quarters
1	bay leaf
6	peppercorns
1	tablespoon salt
1	tablespoon sugar
4	ounces dried mushrooms
12	cups water
3	beets
	Dumplings

Place the carrot, celery, onion, bay leaf, peppercorns, salt, sugar, mushrooms and water in a large kettle. Simmer until the vegetables are tender. Strain the broth, reserving the mushrooms but discarding the vegetables and bay leaf. Chop the mushrooms and set aside to use in the filling for the dumplings. Cook the beets separately until tender; drain, reserving the beet juice. Peel and grate beets coarsely or cut into julienne strips. Place grated beets into soup tureen. Add the strained broth. Add the reserved beet juice to taste. Keep warm. Add Dumplings.

Yield: 8 to 10 servings

Lydia Ringus, Knights of Lithuanian Dancers

DUMPLINGS OR "LITTLE EARS"

Filling

	Chopped mushrooms
1	onion, sliced
2	teaspoons dry bread crumbs
1/2	teaspoon salt
	Dash of pepper
1	egg, beaten

Dough

2	tablespoons oil
1 1/2	cups flour
1	egg
	Salt to taste
1	egg white

Press the mushrooms, onion, bread crumbs, 1/2 teaspoon salt and pepper through a food grinder twice. Add beaten egg and oil, mixing well; set aside. Mix the flour, 1 egg and salt with enough water to make a soft dough. Roll out to 1/8-inch thickness on a floured surface. Cut into 1 1/2-inch squares. Place a teaspoon of the mushroom filling on the dough squares. Brush edges with egg white. Fold diagonally to form a triangle, pressing edges together to seal. Twist two ends of the triangle up and over to form "ears." Drop into boiling water in a kettle. Simmer for 5 minutes. Drain.

BORSCH *Ukraine*
BEET SOUP

8   ounces fresh
    mushrooms, chopped
2   pounds beets, quartered
2   medium onions,
    quartered
2   ribs of celery, sliced
1   carrot, sliced
1   parsnip, sliced
1   turnip, quartered
1   bay leaf
3   to 4 peppercorns
1   quart Kvas (below)
2   teaspoons salt
1   teaspoon freshly
    ground pepper
    Vushka (page 82)
2   teaspoons freshly
    chopped dill

Cook the mushrooms in water to cover in a saucepan until tender. Remove and chop the mushrooms. Reserve the mushroom liquid. Place the beets in a saucepan with water to cover. Cook over low heat for 1 to 2 hours or until tender. Drain and reserve beet liquid. Peel and shred the beets; set aside. Combine the mushrooms and next 7 ingredients in a large kettle with enough water to cover. Cook over low heat until the vegetables are tender. Stir in reserved beet liquid; add the shredded beets. Simmer for 10 minutes. Strain gently into a large stockpot. Add the Kvas, salt and pepper. Stir in reserved mushroom liquid to taste. Bring to a boil; reduce heat to low. Remove bay leaf before serving. To serve, place 2 to 4 Vushka in a soup bowl, add hot borsch and garnish with chopped dill.

Yield: 8 to 10 servings

Ukrainian National Women's League,
Branch 22, in Chicago

This Ukrainian borsch is served with dumplings called "Vushka" and is another variation on beet soup. Three ounces of dried mushrooms may be substituted for the fresh mushrooms but soak them overnight before using. Borsch can be refrigerated for several days. To keep the color from turning brown, do not overcook when reheating.

KVAS

3   pounds beets, peeled,
    cut into quarters
3   tablespoons coarse salt
1   slice sourdough bread

Place the beets in a sterilized 1-gallon glass jar; sprinkle with the coarse salt. Do not use table salt. Pour boiling water over the beets to cover. Let stand to cool. Add the bread. Cover the jar with cheesecloth and secure with string. Let stand in a cool place for 1 week to ferment, skimming off any mold that forms. Taste to see that the mixture is slightly sour. Allow the mixture to ferment a few days longer for desired taste. Discard the cheesecloth and bread and skim off mold. Strain the liquid into sterilized 1-quart jars, discarding the beets. Store, covered, in the refrigerator.

Yield: 4 quarts

Soups & Salads

ZUPA Z/BURAKÓW *Poland*

BEET SOUP

In this variation, a soup bone is used for flavor, and canned beets for ease in preparation.

1	(2-pound) soup bone
1	teaspoon salt
1	bay leaf
3	quarts water
2	(16-ounce) cans beets, drained
1	cup sour cream
2	tablespoons sugar
2	tablespoons flour
3	tablespoons vinegar

Place the soup bone, salt, bay leaf, and water in a soup pot. Cook for 1 hour. Remove from heat and let stand until cool; discard the bone and bay leaf. Combine the beets, sour cream, sugar, flour and vinegar in a blender. Process until smooth. Add to the cooled broth. Bring to a boil; reduce the heat. Simmer until thickened, stirring frequently. Serve with boiled potatoes, hard-boiled eggs and slices of cooked kielbasa sausage.

Yield: 8 to 10 servings

Joan Pitchford, Lansing Business Women's Association

Israel

MEAT BORSCHT

3	quarts water
2	pounds beef brisket
	Beef bones
8	beets, grated
1/2	head of cabbage, shredded
1/2	of a 15-ounce can tomato purée
2	onions, chopped
2	cloves of garlic, minced
1	tablespoon salt
3	tablespoons brown sugar
1/3	cup lemon juice
2	eggs

Bring the water to a boil in a large soup pot. Add the brisket and bones. Continue to boil, skimming the surface frequently. Add the beets, cabbage, tomato purée, onions, garlic and salt. Cook, covered, over medium heat for 2 hours. Add the brown sugar and lemon juice. Simmer for 30 minutes longer. Season to taste. Beat the eggs in a bowl. Add a small amount of the hot soup mixture, beating well to prevent curdling. Add the egg mixture to the soup gradually, stirring constantly. Serve hot.

Yield: 8 to 10 servings

Embassy of Israel and Consulate General of Israel to the Midwest

BORSCHT *Belarus*
BEET SOUP

1 small cabbage, shredded

3 medium beets, cut into julienne strips

3 to 4 medium potatoes, cubed

1 onion, sliced

2 to 3 carrots, sliced

2 green bell peppers, sliced

2 medium tomatoes, sliced

2 to 3 ribs of celery, sliced

1 bay leaf

2 to 3 tablespoons chicken-flavored soup base

1 teaspoon each garlic powder, salt and pepper

Sprinkle the cabbage with salt. Let stand for 2 to 3 minutes. Squeeze until the cabbage is softened; set aside. Combine the beets, potatoes, onion, carrots, green peppers, tomatoes, celery, bay leaf, soup base, garlic powder, salt and pepper in a large stockpot. Add enough water to cover. Cook over medium heat for 45 minutes, stirring occasionally. Add the cabbage. Cook for 15 minutes longer or until the beets become light pink or white, adding water if needed. Season to taste with additional garlic powder and soup base. Remove the bay leaf before serving.

Yield: 6 to 8 servings

Raisa Bratkiv, Bielarusian Coordinating Committee of Chicago

As these variations demonstrate, beet soup can be served hot or cold. When the weather turns warm, Chilled Beet Soup, Chaladnik, can provide a welcome "summer coolant." This refreshing soup is delicious served with hot boiled potatoes or rye bread with or without caraway seeds.

CHALADNIK *Belarus*
CHILLED BEET SOUP

1 (15-ounce) can julienned beets

2 tablespoons fresh dill

1 medium cucumber

4 to 6 green onions, sliced

1 teaspoon salt

1 quart chilled buttermilk

1 cup water

Pour the undrained beets into a 4-quart dish. Chop coarsely with a food chopper. Chop the dill. Peel, seed and dice the cucumber. Add to the beets along with the green onions, dill and salt; stir to mix. Stir in the buttermilk and water. Serve immediately or chill for up to 24 hours.

Yield: 6 to 8 servings

Vera Romuk, Bielarusian Coordinating Committee of Chicago

SOUPS & SALADS

Sweden
FISH SOUP

2	leeks, sliced
4	medium potatoes
1	to 2 ribs celery
2	tablespoons margarine
1	teaspoon each salt and pepper
5	cups water
1	pound fish fillets
1	tablespoon chopped fresh dillweed

Sauté the leeks, cubed potatoes and chopped celery in margarine in a large heavy skillet over low heat for 5 minutes. Add salt, pepper and water. Bring to a boil. Cook for 10 to 15 minutes or until the vegetables are tender. Cut the fish fillets into 1-inch pieces. Add to the soup. Simmer for 10 minutes longer. Sprinkle with dillweed and serve hot.

Yield: 4 servings

Virginia Hast, Linnea South Suburban Swedish Women's Club

Italy
ULTIMATE MINESTRONE

Minestrone, meaning "big soup," is just that—a cross between a soup and a stew.

1	cup chopped onion
1	leek, white part only
4	cloves of garlic, minced
2	tablespoons oil
3 1/2	quarts water
4	ounces prosciutto
2	teaspoons each salt, pepper and sage
	Minestrone Vegetables (at left)
1	cup peas
3	large potatoes, cubed
1/2	to 3/4 cup ditalini macaroni
	Grated Parmesan cheese

Sauté the onion, sliced leek and garlic in oil in a skillet until lightly browned. Bring the water to a boil in a large stockpot. Add the onion mixture, chopped prosciutto, salt, pepper, sage and Minestrone Vegetables. Simmer for 2 1/2 hours, stirring occasionally. Add the peas, potatoes and macaroni. Simmer until the potatoes are tender. Serve with grated Parmesan cheese and garlic bread. May substitute salt pork or bacon for the prosciutto and small soup pasta or rice for the macaroni.

Yield: 8 servings

Mary and Tony Dinolfo

ADAS BIS SILQ *Lebanon*

LENTIL AND SILVERBEET SOUP

1½ cups brown lentils

6 cups cold water

1 large onion, finely chopped

¼ cup olive oil

3 cloves of garlic, minced

8 to 10 silverbeet leaves (Swiss chard)

¼ cup chopped coriander leaves

Salt and pepper to taste

¼ cup lemon juice

Rinse the lentils well. Place in a large, heavy pan with the water. Bring to a boil, skimming the surface; reduce the heat. Simmer, covered, for 1 hour or until the lentils are tender. Brown the onion in oil in a skillet until translucent. Add the garlic. Sauté for 1 minute longer. Rinse the silverbeet leaves and discard the stems. Slice the leaves into halves and coarsely shred. Add to the onion mixture. Cook until the leaves wilt. Add the mixture to the lentils, with the coriander, salt, pepper and lemon juice. Simmer, covered, for 15 to 20 minutes longer. Serve the soup garnished with lemon wedges.

Yield: 5 to 6 servings
Anita Kropp

SOUPS & SALADS

WHEN ANITA THINKS OF THIS SOUP, SHE REMEMBERS COLD WINTER AFTERNOONS COMING HOME FROM SCHOOL TO THE WELCOMING AROMA AND SOOTHING WARMTH OF THIS DELICIOUS SOUP. A GOOD WAY TO MAKE YOU FORGET ALL YOUR HOMEWORK!
THE SILVERBEET IS ALSO KNOWN AS SWISS CHARD. IT IS A MEMBER OF THE BEET FAMILY WITH SILVERY STALKS THAT GIVE IT ITS NAME.

SOUPA FAKIIA *Greece*

LENTIL SOUP

Lentil soup is served as a main course with feta cheese and crusty bread. This soup is also a Lenten dish.

1 pound dried lentils

2 quarts water

½ cup olive oil

1 cup chopped celery

½ cup chopped carrots

1 medium onion, finely chopped

2 tablespoons chopped parsley

1 tablespoon tomato paste

Minced garlic, salt and pepper to taste

Rinse the lentils well. Combine with the water in a 4-quart saucepan. Bring to a boil; reduce the heat. Simmer for 45 minutes or until the lentils are tender. Add the olive oil, celery, carrots, onion, parsley, tomato paste, garlic, salt and pepper. Simmer until the vegetables are tender.

Yield: 6 to 8 servings
Anna Livaditis, Peiraikon Hellenic School

A SEASON OF CELEBRATING

Soups & Salads

THERE ARE MANY LEGENDS ABOUT HOW THE LEEK CAME TO BE ONE OF THE NATIONAL EMBLEMS OF WALES. ONE POPULAR ONE IS THAT ST. DAVID, THE PATRON SAINT OF WALES, ADVISED THE BRITONS, ON THE EVE OF A BATTLE WITH THE SAXONS, TO WEAR LEEKS IN THEIR CAPS SO AS TO EASILY DISTINGUISH THEIR FRIENDS FROM THEIR FOES. THIS HELPED THEM TO WIN A GREAT VICTORY. AS A RESULT, LEEKS ARE TRADITIONALLY WORN ON ST. DAVID'S DAY, MARCH 1.

NAMED AFTER THE ISLAND PROVINCE NOTED FOR THE HIGH QUALITY OF ITS POTATOES, THIS SOUP REPRESENTS A COMPROMISE BETWEEN THAT MADE WITH MEAT STOCK BY THE HOMESTEADERS AND THE MODERN CREAM OF POTATO SOUP. BEEF OR CHICKEN STOCK MAY BE SUBSTITUTED FOR THE WATER.

Wales
LEEK SOUP

1	to 2 cups sliced leeks
3	tablespoons butter
4	cups cold water
1	bay leaf
2	tablespoons chili sauce
2	chicken bouillon cubes
2	medium potatoes, cubed
1/2	small onion, chopped
1/3	cup finely chopped carrot
1/3	cup chopped celery
2	tablespoons chopped parsley
1	cup milk

Sauté the leeks in butter in a large heavy saucepan until tender-crisp. Add the cold water, bay leaf, chili sauce and bouillon cubes, stirring well. Add the potatoes, onion, carrot, celery and parsley. Simmer over medium heat until the vegetables are tender. Stir in the milk. Cook over low heat until heated through. Thicken the soup with cornstarch if desired. Discard the bay leaf before serving.

Yield: 4 to 5 servings

Ann Williams, Cambrian Benevolent Society of Chicago

Canada
P.E.I. POTATO SOUP

3	cups water
1	teaspoon salt
3	to 4 medium potatoes, cut into quarters
1	(16-ounce) can evaporated milk
1	tablespoon grated onion
3	tablespoons butter
	Salt and pepper to taste
1/2	cup shredded cheese

Bring the water and 1 teaspoon salt to a boil in a heavy saucepan. Add the potatoes. Simmer, covered, for 25 minutes or until the potatoes are tender. Drain, reserving the cooking liquid. Press the potatoes through a sieve. Mix the reserved cooking liquid, evaporated milk, onion, butter and pepper in a saucepan. Heat gently until the butter melts; do not boil. Add the potatoes. Simmer until heated through, adding additional water for desired consistency. Season with salt and pepper to taste. Stir in the cheese. Simmer until the cheese melts. Garnish with chopped parsley.

Yield: 6 servings

The Canadian Women's Club of Chicago

ÄRTER MED FLÄSK *Sweden*
PEA SOUP WITH PORK

1½ cups dried yellow
  Swedish peas

2½ quarts water

1 pound lightly-salted
  side pork or 2 pounds
  fresh pork shoulder
  with bone

2 medium onions, sliced

½ teaspoon powdered
  ginger

1 teaspoon leaf marjoram

  Salt and pepper to taste

Sort and rinse the peas. Place in a 4-quart saucepan with the water. Soak for 8 to 10 hours; do not change the water. Cover and bring to a boil, removing any shells that float to the surface. Cook for 2 hours. Add the pork, onions, ginger and marjoram. Simmer, covered, over low heat for 1 hour or until the pork is cooked through and the peas are tender. Season with salt and pepper. Remove the pork. Slice thinly and serve separately with mustard.

Yield: 4 servings

Aina Momquist, Linnea South Suburban Swedish Women's Club

ERBSENSUPPE *Germany*
SPLIT PEA SOUP

Rich, nourishing soups are popular in Germany as one-dish meals when served with good dark bread and beer.

1 pound dried split peas

5 quarts water

2 pounds smoked beef
  shanks

1 medium onion,
  chopped

1 clove of garlic, crushed

4 carrots, chopped

1½ cups chopped celery

1 tablespoon chopped
  fresh parsley

3 potatoes, cubed

1 tablespoon salt

3 bay leaves

Sort and rinse the peas. Bring the water to a boil in a stockpot. Add the beef shanks. Cook for 2½ hours or until the meat is tender. Remove the beef with a slotted spoon to a bowl, reserving the liquid. Shred the beef, discarding the bones. Add the peas, onion, garlic, carrots, celery, parsley, potatoes, salt and bay leaves to the reserved liquid. Simmer for 1 hour. Stir in the shredded meat. Discard the bay leaves. Dried split peas do not need to be soaked overnight, as do dried whole peas.

Yield: 8 servings

Katherina Scheero, Society of the Danube Swabians

SOUPS & SALADS

PEA SOUP WITH PORK IS CONSIDERED THE NATIONAL DISH OF SWEDEN. IT HAS BEEN SERVED FOR OVER 400 YEARS AND IS FAMILIARLY KNOWN AS "THURSDAY SOUP." BOTH ECONOMICAL AND FILLING, IT IS PARTICULARLY COMFORTING DURING THE COLD WINTER MONTHS. THE SOUP IS USUALLY FOLLOWED BY A SERVING OF PANCAKES, OR "PLÄTTAR" (PAGE 107), TOPPED WITH JAM OR LINGONBERRIES.

SOUPS & SALADS

DURING THE TWELVE DAYS OF CHRISTMAS, WHEN THE FREEZING WINTER TEMPERATURES CAUSE ICE TO FORM ON THE CANALS IN THE NETHERLANDS, COSTUMED GROUPS GATHER FOR RACES AND ICE CELEBRATIONS. WHEREVER THERE IS ICE SKATING THERE ARE ALSO VENDORS SELLING WARM FOOD AND DRINKS. THE SKATERS WARM UP WITH A STEAMING CUP OF ERWTENSOEP, THE DUTCH PEA SOUP (ALSO CALLED "SNERT") AND WARM ANISE-FLAVORED MILK BEFORE HOPPING TO THE NEXT CANAL TO CONTINUE SKATING.

———

THE WHOLE YELLOW PEAS IN THIS RECIPE DO REQUIRE SOAKING BEFORE USE. SOME OF THE INGREDIENTS ARE SIMILAR TO OTHER PEA SOUP RECIPES, HOWEVER, THIS ONE USES DIFFERENT HERBS AND IS PURÉED. IT IS TRADITIONALLY SERVED FOR A MIDNIGHT CHRISTMAS MEAL IN THE FRENCH-SPEAKING PROVINCES OF CANADA.

ERWTENSOEP *The Netherlands*
SPLIT PEA SOUP

16	ounces dried green split peas
3	quarts water
1	small ham shank
1	large onion, chopped
2	chicken bouillon cubes
$1/2$	teaspoon garlic powder
$1/2$	teaspoon dried oregano
$1/2$	teaspoon freshly ground Five Blend Pepper
1	bay leaf
$1^1/2$	cups thinly sliced carrots
1	cup chopped celery

Sort and rinse the peas. Combine the peas, water, ham shank, onion, bouillon cubes, garlic powder, oregano, pepper and bay leaf in a 5-quart saucepan. Bring to a boil; reduce heat. Simmer for $1^1/2$ hours. Remove the ham shank and trim the meat from the bone. Add the ham, carrots and celery to the soup. Simmer for 2 to $2^1/2$ hours longer or until of desired consistency. Discard the bay leaf.

Yield: 6 servings

Margie Rysner, The Chicago Museum Committee

SOUPE AUX POIS *Canada*
FRENCH CANADIAN PEA SOUP

2	cups dried whole yellow peas
12	cups cold water
	Salt pork or ham bone
1	cup chopped onion
$1/2$	cup chopped celery
$1/2$	cup chopped carrot
	Pinch of savory and parsley
1	bay leaf
2	teaspoons salt (optional)
$1/4$	teaspoon pepper
1	cup cubed potatoes

Sort and rinse the peas. Soak for 8 to 10 hours in 4 cups of the cold water in a stockpot. Add the remaining 8 cups of cold water, salt pork, onion, celery, carrot, savory, parsley, bay leaf, salt and pepper. Bring to a boil; reduce the heat. Simmer, covered, for 2 hours or until the peas are tender. Add the potatoes. Cook for 15 minutes longer. Remove and discard the salt pork and bay leaf. Purée the soup in a blender until of the desired consistency, processing only a small amount at a time. Reheat before serving.

Yield: 8 to 10 servings

The Canadian Women's Club of Chicago

MISO OZONI (KYOTO-STYLE) *Japan*
RICE CAKE AND BOILED VEGETABLES

1/2   carrot, peeled

1/2   daikon (white radish), peeled

2   sato imo (taro potatoes), peeled

4   cups water

2   teaspoons Hon-Dashi (soup stock)

1/4   cup white miso (soybean paste)

4   to 8 mochi (small plain rice cakes), steamed

Slice the carrot, daikon and sato imo into 1/4-inch rounds. Bring the water to a boil in a large saucepan. Stir in the Hon-Dashi. Add the sliced vegetables. Simmer until the vegetables are tender. Stir a small amount of the soup stock into the miso to thin. Add to the stock. Bring to a boil; turn off heat. Place the mochi in a large soup bowl. Arrange the cooked vegetables over the steamed mochi; cover with the soup stock. Garnish with spinach or shingiku (edible chrysanthemum).

Yield: 4 servings
Tampopo-Kai

OZONI, A SOUP OF VEGETABLES OR CHICKEN SERVED OVER MOCHI (RICE CAKES), IS TRADITIONALLY THE FIRST DISH SERVED ON NEW YEAR'S MORNING IN JAPAN TO WISH GOOD HEALTH AND PROSPERITY TO ALL. THE FOLLOWING ARE VARIATIONS OF OZONI FROM THREE DIFFERENT REGIONS. TO COOK THE MOCHI, PLACE THEM IN A PAN OF HOT WATER AND STEAM FOR 1 MINUTE OR UNTIL SOFT.

SUMASHI OZONI (TOKYO-STYLE) *Japan*
RICE CAKE, CHICKEN AND BOILED VEGETABLES

4   dried shiitake mushrooms

1/2   carrot

8   snow peas or mizuna

4   cups water

4   ounces boneless chicken, cut into bite-size pieces

2   teaspoons Hon-Dashi (soup stock)

1   teaspoon salt

1   teaspoon soy sauce

4   to 8 mochi (small plain rice cakes), steamed

4   to 8 kamaboko (fish cakes), sliced

Soak the mushrooms in warm water for 30 minutes; drain and pat dry. Remove the stems and slice into halves. Slice the carrot into 1-inch lengths. Slice down, but not all the way through, several times, and press down firmly to form a flower. Parboil the carrot and snow peas in a saucepan. Bring the water to a boil in a saucepan. Add the chicken. Boil for 2 to 3 minutes, skimming off the foam. Add the Hon-Dashi and mushrooms. Bring to a boil. Stir in the salt and soy sauce. Place the cooked mochi in a soup bowl. Arrange the carrot flowers, kamaboko and snow peas on top and cover with the soup broth.

Yield: 4 servings
Tampopo-Kai

KOREA ALSO SERVES ITS OWN
VERSION OF RICE CAKE SOUP
ON NEW YEAR'S DAY. THIS
ONE IS PREPARED USING BEEF.
KOREAN CHEFS OFTEN
GARNISH SOUPS WITH A PAPER-
THIN FRIED EGG SLICED INTO
STRIPS OR DIAMOND SHAPES.

SATSUMA ZONI (KYUSHU-STYLE) *Japan*

RICE CAKE, CHICKEN AND BOILED VEGETABLES

4	large sato imo (taro potatoes)
4	cups water
1	boneless chicken breast, sliced into $1/4$-inch strips
$1^1/_2$	teaspoons Hon-Dashi (soup stock)
$1/4$	cup shiro miso (white soybean paste)
4	ounces bean sprouts
4	to 8 mochi (small plain rice cakes)

Parboil the sato imo in a saucepan; drain. Let stand until cool. Peel and cut into $1/2$-inch slices. Bring the water to a boil in a saucepan. Add the chicken. Cook for 2 to 3 minutes. Add the Hon-Dashi, miso and sato imo. Simmer until the sato imo are tender. Add the bean sprouts and mochi. Simmer until the mochi are soft. Remove the mochi with a slotted spoon and place in a large soup bowl. Top with the vegetables and cover with the soup.

Yield: 4 servings

Tampopo-Kai

DUK GUK *Korea*

RICE CAKE SOUP

2	ounces lean beef, finely chopped
$1/2$	clove of garlic, finely crushed
$1/2$	teaspoon soy sauce
$1/4$	teaspoon sesame oil
$1/8$	teaspoon pepper
1	quart water
1	(1-pound) frozen rice cake, sliced
1	green onion, sliced
1	egg

Stir-fry the beef and garlic with the soy sauce, sesame oil and pepper in a 2-quart saucepan until the beef is browned. Add the water. Bring to a boil; reduce heat to low. Simmer for 10 to 15 minutes. Increase the heat to high and bring to a boil. Rinse the rice cake; drain. Add to the broth. Cook for 5 minutes or until the rice cake is tender. Remove from heat. Garnish with the green onion and egg. The egg may be quickly stirred in, or cooked and finely chopped.

Yield: 4 servings

Alycia Wright and Alice Jung

UJHÁZI LEVES AND MÁJAS GOMBOC *Hungary*

CHICKEN SOUP WITH LIVER DUMPLINGS

2   (2-pound) chickens
    with giblets

3   or 4 carrots, sliced

2   parsley roots, sliced

1   small head cauliflower,
    separated

1   bunch fresh parsley,
    coarsely chopped

1   small head savoy
    cabbage, shredded

1   bay leaf

1   onion, studded with
    cloves

1   teaspoon tarragon

1   teaspoon marjoram

1   clove of garlic, chopped

$1/2$ teaspoon white
    peppercorns

$1/2$ teaspoon black
    peppercorns

    Salt to taste

$3/4$ to 1 cup fresh green
    peas

8   ounces fresh
    mushrooms, sliced

    Liver Dumplings
    (at right)

Cut the chicken into serving pieces and chop the giblets. Combine with the carrots, parsley roots, cauliflower, parsley, cabbage, bay leaf, onion, tarragon, marjoram, garlic, peppercorns, salt, peas and mushrooms in a 6-quart stockpot. Add enough water to cover. Bring to a boil; reduce heat to medium. Simmer for $1^1/2$ to 2 hours or until the chicken is cooked through and the vegetables are tender. Transfer to a soup tureen, discarding the bay leaf. Add the Liver Dumplings and serve.

Yield: 8 to 10 servings

Calvin Reformed Church of Lynwood, Illinois

UJHÁZI SOUP IS NAMED IN HONOR OF THE ACTOR EDE UJHÁZI (1844–1915), AN ACTOR WHO PIONEERED THE MODERN, REALISTIC STYLE OF ACTING.

FOR THE LIVER DUMPLINGS, GRIND OR FINELY CHOP 6 CHICKEN LIVERS OR 8 OUNCES CALVES LIVER. COMBINE WITH $1/2$ TEASPOON SALT, $1/2$ TEASPOON CHOPPED PARSLEY, 2 BEATEN EGGS AND 2 TABLESPOONS WATER IN A BOWL. ADD 1 CUP FLOUR, STIRRING TO FORM A SOFT DOUGH. BRING 2 QUARTS OF SALTED WATER TO A BOIL. DROP IN THE DOUGH BY $1/4$ TEASPOONFULS. COOK FOR 5 MINUTES OR UNTIL THE DUMPLINGS RISE TO THE TOP. REMOVE WITH A SLOTTED SPOON TO A COLANDER. RINSE WITH COLD WATER AND DRAIN. SERVE IN THE CHICKEN SOUP.

SOUPS & SALADS

IN CHINA, SOUP MAY BE SERVED AS A BEVERAGE. FOR IMPORTANT DINNERS, IT IS USUALLY SERVED AT THE END OF THE MEAL. THIS DISH IS FROM THE SHANGHAI REGION AND IS OFTEN SERVED FOR BIRTHDAYS. THE NOODLES SYMBOLIZE LONG LIFE.

———

RINDFLEISCH-SUPPE IS THE DANUBE SWABIAN VERSION OF A BOILED, ONE-POT DINNER THAT WAS THE FIRST COURSE OF THE SUNDAY MEAL.

China
CHICKEN NOODLE STEW

1	pound noodles
2	tablespoons oil
2	cups shredded green cabbage
1/4	cup shredded ham
2	cups cooked sliced chicken
1/4	cup sliced mushrooms
1/2	cup stock
2	teaspoons salt
1	tablespoon cornstarch
2	tablespoons water
2	quarts chicken stock

Cook the noodles in boiling salted water in a saucepan for 5 minutes; drain. Heat the oil in a wok or skillet. Stir-fry the cabbage in the hot oil for 3 minutes. Add the ham, chicken and mushrooms. Pour in 1/2 cup stock; add 2 teaspoons salt. Dissolve the cornstarch in the water. Stir into the chicken mixture. Bring 2 quarts stock to a boil in a saucepan. Add the noodles and the chicken mixture. Adjust the seasonings. Serve hot.

Yield: 4 servings

Ginger Cheung, Chinese American Civic Council

RINDFLEISCH-SUPPE *Germany*
BEEF BROTH SOUP

1 1/2	pounds stew beef
1	soup bone
1	onion, quartered
2	carrots, sliced
	Parsley to taste
1	tomato, chopped
1/2	green bell pepper, sliced
2	ribs celery, sliced
1	clove of garlic, minced
2	quarts water
2	teaspoons salt
6	peppercorns
6	whole cloves
1	bay leaf

Combine the stew beef, soup bone, onion, carrots, parsley, tomato, green pepper, celery, garlic and water in a 4-quart saucepan. Add the salt, peppercorns, cloves and bay leaf. Bring to a boil; reduce heat. Simmer for 2 hours or until the beef is tender. Remove the meat and the vegetables with a slotted spoon to a heated platter. Strain the broth, discarding the peppercorns, cloves and bay leaf. Serve the meat with boiled potatoes and dill sauce and add Liver Dumplings (page 35), noodles or griess knödel to the beef broth.

Yield: 8 servings

Society of the Danube Swabians

Denmark

Danish Soup with Meatballs and Dumplings

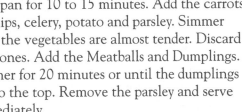

1 1/2 pounds beef marrow bones

3 or 4 carrots, peeled, sliced

2 or 3 medium parsnips, peeled, sliced

3 to 4 ribs celery, sliced

1 potato, peeled, sliced

1 large bunch parsley, tied with string

Meatballs (at right)

Dumplings (at right)

Cook the bones in 2 quarts water in a 4-quart saucepan for 10 to 15 minutes. Add the carrots, parsnips, celery, potato and parsley. Simmer until the vegetables are almost tender. Discard the bones. Add the Meatballs and Dumplings. Simmer for 20 minutes or until the dumplings rise to the top. Remove the parsley and serve immediately.

Yield: 6 to 8 servings

Margaret V. Tredon, Danish Sisterhood Society, Olga Lodge 11

Groentesoep met Gehakt Balletjes *The Netherlands*

Vegetable Soup with Meatballs

3 or 4 ribs celery, finely chopped

2 or 3 carrots, chopped

2 small leeks or green onions, chopped

2 ounces Dutch vermicelli or thin spaghetti

1/4 cup rice

5 beef or chicken bouillon cubes

2 packages vegetable soup mix

Vegetable Soup Meatballs (at right)

Bring 2 to 3 quarts of water to a boil in a large saucepan. Add the celery, carrots, leeks, vermicelli and rice. Simmer for 1 1/2 hours over medium heat. Add the bouillon cubes, soup mix and Vegetable Soup Meatballs. Simmer for 15 minutes longer. Season to taste. The soup is best when served the next day.

Yield: 6 to 8 servings

Henny Bos, Chicago Museum Committee

Soups & Salads

For the meatballs in Danish Soup, combine 8 ounces lean ground beef, 1/2 teaspoon salt and 1/4 teaspoon pepper in a bowl. Add 1 to 2 tablespoons flour to hold the mixture together. Shape into 1-inch balls.

For the dumplings, bring 1/2 cup water to a boil in a heavy saucepan. Add 1/2 cup flour all at once, stirring until the mixture leaves the side of the pan. Remove from heat. Stir in 1 unbeaten egg. Shape the dumplings with a spoon dipped in the soup broth.

To prepare the Vegetable Soup Meatballs, mix 1 pound ground beef, 1/4 cup bread crumbs, 1/8 teaspoon each salt, pepper, cloves, nutmeg and allspice, and 1 beaten egg in a bowl. Add a small amount of milk if needed. Shape into 1-inch balls.

"BLESSING THE DANUBE" IS A TIME-HONORED ROMANIAN CUSTOM. PEOPLE DRESS IN COSTUMES TO DEPICT PONTIUS PILATE, HEROD AND OTHER BIBLICAL CHARACTERS WHILE GATHERING AT THE RIVER BANK TO SING CAROLS.

Romania
MEATBALL SOUP

4	cups chicken stock
2	teaspoons medium-hot salsa
2	onions, chopped
1	carrot, finely chopped
1	small celery root, finely chopped
1	parsley root, finely chopped
1	small parsnip, finely chopped
	Meatballs
1	cup tomato juice
1	tablespoon lemon juice
1	teaspoon flat-leaf parsley, finely chopped
1	teaspoon fresh dillweed, finely chopped

Combine the chicken stock, salsa, onions, carrot, celery root, parsley root and parsnip in a 4-quart saucepan. Bring to a boil; reduce the heat to medium. Simmer for 30 minutes while preparing the meatballs. Add the meatballs; reduce the heat to low. Simmer for 15 minutes. Stir in the tomato juice and lemon juice; season to taste. Simmer for 10 minutes longer; remove from the heat. Sprinkle with the parsley and dillweed. Cover and let stand until ready to serve.

Yield: 4 to 6 servings
The Romanian Christmas Group Holy Nativity

MEATBALLS

1	onion, finely chopped
2	tablespoons olive oil
2	tablespoons rice (rinsed)
3	tablespoons soup stock
1	pound ground beef
1	slice bread, cubed
1	egg, beaten

Sauté the onion in the olive oil in a small skillet until the onion is lightly browned. Add the rice. Stir-fry for 2 to 3 minutes. Add the soup stock. Simmer for 5 minutes or until the rice is softened; cool. Combine with the ground beef, bread and egg in a medium bowl, mixing well. Shape into 1-inch balls. Add to the soup stock.

Belarus

CABBAGE SALAD

6 pounds cabbage, shredded

3 carrots, shredded

1 clove of garlic, crushed

1½ quarts water

½ cup sugar

1 cup oil

1 bay leaf

¼ cup salt

1 cup vinegar

Mix the cabbage, carrots and garlic in a large bowl. Combine the water, sugar, oil, bay leaf and salt in a large saucepan. Bring to a boil; remove from the heat. Pour over the cabbage mixture. Stir in the vinegar. Let stand for 15 to 20 minutes. Stir well and let stand, covered, at room temperature for 2 to 3 days, stirring occasionally. Discard the bay leaf. Spoon into sterilized glass jars. Store in the refrigerator.

Yield: 8 to 10 servings

Elizabeth Kulas, Bielarusian Coordinating Committee of Chicago

SOMETIMES IN BELARUS, FAMILIES WILL INVITE A STRANDED TRAVELLER OR A HOMELESS PERSON TO SHARE THE MEAL WITH THEM. AFTER THE MEAL IS OVER, THE FAMILY ENGAGES IN SINGING CAROLS AND FORETELLING THE FUTURE.

Hungary

CUCUMBER SALAD

4 large cucumbers, peeled, thinly sliced

1 medium sweet onion, thinly sliced

Salt to taste

1 tablespoon sugar

1 tablespoon white vinegar

Dash of hot paprika

1 tablespoon szegedi (mild Hungarian paprika)

4 heaping tablespoons sour cream

Combine the cucumbers, onion and salt in a bowl. Chill for 1 hour. Mix the sugar, vinegar, paprika and sour cream in a small bowl. Drain the cucumber mixture well. Add the sour cream mixture to the cucumbers, stirring to coat. Chill before serving.

Yield: 6 servings

Barbara Kaffka, Calvin Reformed Church of Lynwood, Illinois

Soups & Salads

Germany
POTATO SALAD

4	ounces bacon, chopped
1	cup chopped onion
5	pounds potatoes, boiled, peeled, sliced
1/2	cup white wine vinegar
1/2	cup vegetable oil
2	tablespoons prepared mustard
2	cups chicken broth (skimmed)
1/4	cup minced chives or parsley
	Salt and pepper to taste

Fry the bacon in a skillet until almost crisp. Add the onion. Sauté until the onion is translucent and the bacon is crisp; drain well. Combine the bacon mixture with the potatoes in a large bowl. Combine the vinegar, oil, mustard, chicken broth, chives, salt and pepper in a small bowl and mix well. Pour over the potato mixture, tossing to coat. Serve warm.

Yield: 10 servings

Donna Lively, Lansing Business Women's Association

HORIATIKI SALATA *Greece*
VILLAGE SALAD

Salads accompany every Greek dinner and are also served as a complete meal with crusty bread and wine.

1	pound tomatoes, chopped
1	cucumber, chopped
2	onions, finely chopped
1	clove of garlic, minced
1	rib of celery, chopped
	Salt and pepper to taste
	Juice of 1/2 lemon

Arrange the tomatoes and cucumber in a glass salad bowl. Combine the onions, garlic, celery, salt, pepper and lemon juice in a small bowl. Pour over the tomato mixture. Garnish with crumbled feta cheese, kalamata olives and sardines.

Yield: 4 servings

Sophie Liambotis, Peiraikon Hellenic School

PERSIMMON AND VEGETABLE SALAD

1   Japanese cucumber,
     unpeeled
1   rib of celery
1   carrot, peeled
1   daikon (white radish),
     peeled
$1/2$ teaspoon salt
1   fuyu kaki (Japanese
     winter persimmon)
1   teaspoon sugar
$1/4$ cup vinegar
1   tablespoon sugar
1   tablespoon soy sauce

Cut the cucumber, celery, carrot and daikon into 2-inch lengths; slice thinly. Place in a shallow dish; sprinkle with the salt. Let stand for 30 minutes. Squeeze gently to remove water. Peel the persimmon and slice thinly. Sprinkle with 1 teaspoon sugar. Add to the cucumber mixture. Combine the vinegar, 1 tablespoon sugar and soy sauce in a small bowl; mix well. Pour over the cucumber mixture, tossing gently to coat.

Yield: 2 to 4 servings
Tampopo-Kai

SOUPS & SALADS

FOR CENTURIES, ASIAN CHEFS HAVE BEEN USING VEGETABLES AND SEASONING INGREDIENTS THAT WERE RELATIVELY UNKNOWN TO THE REST OF THE WORLD, BUT WHICH ARE NOW BECOMING READILY AVAILABLE. SOME OF THE MOST POPULAR ARE LOTUS ROOT, BOK CHOY, FERMENTED BLACK BEANS, DRIED KELP, BEAN THREAD AND BEAN SPROUTS, AND LYCHEES.

———

LOTUS ROOT WITH SWEET VINEGAR DRESSING

5   tablespoons rice
     vinegar
1   to $1^1/2$ tablespoons
     sugar
     MSG to taste
1   renkon (lotus root)

Combine the rice vinegar, sugar and MSG in a saucepan. Bring to a boil; remove from the heat. Let stand to cool. Wash the renkon and slice crosswise into $1/4$-inch slices. Pare each slice around the holes to form a blossom shape. Place the lotus root blossoms in water to cover in a saucepan. Add a few drops of additional vinegar. Cook the lotus root blossoms for 2 minutes; drain. Place in a bowl. Pour the amazu (rice vinegar dressing) over the lotus root. Marinate in the refrigerator for 8 to 10 hours before serving.

Yield: 2 to 4 servings
Tampopo-Kai

RENKON IS A LOVELY AND DELICATE SALAD. WHEN WORKING WITH THE LOTUS ROOT, SOAK SLICES IN A SOLUTION OF WATER AND VINEGAR TO PREVENT DISCOLORATION. RINSE AND DRAIN THEM BEFORE PROCEEDING. FRESH LOTUS ROOT WILL KEEP FOR 2 WEEKS IN THE REFRIGERATOR.

RAITHA OR RAITA IS THE
TERM USED FOR VEGETABLES,
RAW OR COOKED, WHICH
HAVE BEEN MIXED WITH
SEASONED YOGURT. THIS DISH
IS PART OF THE TRADITIONAL
INDIAN MEAL.

VINEGRETT *Belarus*

BEET, POTATO, KRAUT AND BEAN SALAD

This salad is traditionally served during the Christmas Eve meal in Belarus.

6	medium beets
4	medium potatoes
2	cups sauerkraut
2	medium onions, thinly sliced
6	gherkin pickles
1	(8-ounce) can kidney beans, drained
1	teaspoon salt
1	teaspoon pepper
1/4	to 1/2 cup vegetable oil

Cook the beets in boiling water in a saucepan until tender; cool. Peel and cut into cubes. Cook the potatoes in boiling water until tender; cool. Peel and cut into cubes. Squeeze the sauerkraut to remove all liquid; cut into short strands. Combine the beets, potatoes, sauerkraut, onions, pickles and kidney beans in a large bowl. Season with salt and pepper. Pour the oil over the vegetable mixture, stirring to coat.

Yield: 6 servings

Sofia Latuszkin, Belarusian American National Council of Chicago

RAITHA *India*

YOGURT SALAD

2	cucumbers, peeled
2	large tomatoes, finely chopped
1	(1-inch long) fresh green chile, chopped
1	(1/2-inch) piece gingerroot, minced
1	medium onion, finely chopped
1	small bunch cilantro (coriander leaves), minced
32	ounces plain yogurt
1/4	teaspoon ground cumin
	Salt to taste

Cut the cucumbers into halves; remove the seeds. Chop the cucumbers finely. Combine with the tomatoes, green chile, gingerroot, onion and cilantro in a large bowl. Add the yogurt, stirring gently to mix. Stir in the cumin and salt. Serve chilled, garnished with cilantro leaves.

Yield: 4 to 6 servings

Mariette Rao, India Catholic Association of America

Romania

POTATO, CHICKEN AND VEGETABLE SALAD

4	potatoes
2	tablespoons prepared Italian dressing
2	carrots, chopped
1	celery root, chopped
2	chicken breasts
1½	cups chicken stock
1	(8-ounce) can tiny peas, drained
3	dill pickles, drained, cubed
¾	cup mayonnaise
¼	cup mustard
1	teaspoon lemon juice
¼	teaspoon salt
	Lettuce leaves

Boil the potatoes until tender. Peel and cut into ¼-inch cubes. Place in a bowl and drizzle with the Italian dressing. Marinate for 2 hours, turning to coat. Simmer the carrots, celery root and chicken breasts in the chicken stock in a saucepan until the chicken is cooked through; drain. Chop or shred the chicken coarsely. Place the vegetables and chicken in a large bowl. Drain the marinade from the potatoes. Add the potatoes, peas and pickles to the chicken mixture. Mix the mayonnaise, mustard, lemon juice and salt in a small bowl. Stir into the vegetable mixture gently. Line a large platter with the lettuce leaves. Spoon the salad into the center of the platter. Garnish with sliced carrots, cucumbers and radishes.

Yield: 4 to 6 servings
The Romanian Christmas Group Holy Nativity

SOUPS & SALADS

THE CULTIVATION OF BEAN SPROUTS WAS DEVELOPED BY THE CHINESE. THE METHOD INVOLVES PLACING DRIED SOY BEANS ON BAMBOO TRAYS AND COVERING THEM WITH DAMP CLOTHS. AFTER DAILY TENDING, THE BEAN SPROUTS BEGIN TO APPEAR.

China

SHREDDED CHICKEN, HAM AND BEAN SPROUT SALAD

1	pound bean sprouts
2	quarts boiling water
½	cup shredded ham
1	cup shredded, cooked chicken
1	tablespoon soy sauce
1½	teaspoons vinegar
2	teaspoons sugar
1	teaspoon sesame oil

Rinse the bean sprouts well, pinching off the ends. Place in a colander. Pour the boiling water over them. Rinse with cold water for 2 minutes; drain well. Place in a bowl. Chill in the refrigerator. Add the ham, chicken, soy sauce, vinegar, sugar and sesame oil, tossing to mix. Serve cold.

Yield: 6 servings
Ginger Cheung, Chinese American Civic Council

SOUPS & SALADS

THE RECIPE FOR CODFISH SALAD IS AN OLD-FASHIONED FAMILY FAVORITE FROM ITALY THAT IS SERVED AS PART OF THE MEATLESS CHRISTMAS EVE SUPPER THAT IS COMPOSED PRIMARILY OF FISH.

SALATA Z KURYCY *Belarus*

EASY CHICKEN SALAD

2	cups chopped, cooked chicken
1/2	cup finely chopped celery
1/4	cup prepared French dressing
1/4	cup mayonnaise
1/8	teaspoon cayenne
	Salad greens
	Tomato wedges

Combine the chicken, celery, French dressing, mayonnaise and cayenne in a bowl. Toss to coat. Line salad plates with the salad greens. Spoon the chicken mixture onto the center of each plate. Surround with tomato wedges.

Yield: 4 servings

Marta Kuczura, Bielarusian Coordinating Committee of Chicago

Italy

CHRISTMAS CODFISH SALAD

1	pound dried, salted codfish
2	cups chopped green and red bell peppers
1	cup vinegar
2	cups water
1/2	teaspoon sugar
	Chopped celery leaves and tender stalks
	Chopped parsley
1	(8-ounce) can pitted black olives, drained
3/4	cup olive oil
3/4	cup white wine vinegar
	Juice and grated peel of 1 lemon
2	cloves of garlic, minced
	Oregano to taste

Soak the codfish in water to cover in a pan for 3 to 5 hours, changing the water occasionally; drain. Parboil in a small amount of water in a saucepan for 5 to 7 minutes or until the fish flakes easily. Drain and cool. Boil the green and red peppers in a mixture of 1 cup vinegar, 2 cups water, sugar and a dash of salt in a saucepan for 2 to 3 minutes. Remove from the heat and let stand to cool; drain. Combine the codfish, peppers, celery, parsley and olives in a large bowl. Whisk the olive oil with 3/4 cup vinegar, lemon juice and peel, garlic, oregano, salt and pepper to taste in a small bowl. Pour 3/4 of the dressing over the cod mixture, tossing gently to coat. Chill for 24 hours. Drizzle with the remaining dressing before serving.

Yield: 6 to 8 servings

Evelyn Devivo Meine

CHAPTER Three

MAIN DISHES

A SEASON *of* CELEBRATING

Diwali

⟨⟨⟨⟩⟩⟩

The Diwali festival is a very happy time for the people of India, including the Hindus and Sikhs. The festival is actually a series of holidays celebrated in late October or early November. During one Diwali holiday, families share special foods, including a dinner featuring fourteen different dishes. Indian homes are decorated with thousands of dipas (oil burning lamps) that glow and gleam throughout the country. One Diwali celebration honors the legend of Rama, the son of a beloved king. Rama was sent away by his evil stepmother for fourteen years so she could plot to have her own son made king. Eventually, Rama returned home with the help of the people of India who lit thousands of dipas to light his way.

BUL GO KI *Korea*
BARBECUED BEEF

1   pound beef tenderloin or flank steak

2   tablespoons sugar

2   tablespoons rice wine

2¹/₂ tablespoons soy sauce

1   clove of garlic, crushed

¹/₂   teaspoon crushed gingerroot

2   green onions, chopped

1   teaspoon toasted sesame seeds, slightly pounded

¹/₈   teaspoon pepper

1   tablespoon water

Slice the beef against the grain into thin slices and place in a large shallow dish. Sprinkle with 1 tablespoon of the sugar and 1 tablespoon of the rice wine. Stir the beef to coat. Marinate for 10 to 15 minutes. Combine the remaining sugar, the remaining rice wine, soy sauce, garlic, gingerroot, green onions, sesame seeds, pepper and water in a bowl; mix well. Pour the sauce over the beef, turning to coat. Marinate for 15 minutes longer. Grill the beef over hot coals or oven-broil at 450 degrees for 1 minute on each side or until browned.

Yield: 6 servings
Alycia Wright and Alice Jung

FATTA *Egypt*
BREAD, RICE AND BEEF

This is a traditional dish served in Egypt at Christmas and Easter. The pita bread may be fried slightly before soaking for extra flavor.

4   to 6 pita breads, cut into bite-sized pieces

    Beef broth

2   cups cooked rice

1   to 2 pounds beef stew meat, cooked

1   tablespoon melted butter or margarine

2   to 3 cloves of garlic, minced

Place the pita bread in a large shallow serving dish. Pour in enough broth to cover the bread. Let stand until the liquid is absorbed. Layer the rice and beef over the pita. Combine the melted butter and the garlic; pour over the beef layer. Serve immediately.

Yield: 6 servings
Mary N. Khair, St. Mark's Coptic Church

MAIN DISHES

MARINATED BEEF ROAST

To tenderize and flavor meats, Germans often use marinades composed of wine, vinegar, herbs and spices, such as found in this recipe for Sauerbraten.

5	pounds rump sirloin roast
2	cups red wine vinegar
2	cups water
2	onions, sliced
1	lemon, sliced
10	whole cloves
4	bay leaves
6	peppercorns
2	teaspoons salt
1	tablespoon sugar
2	teaspoons butter or margarine
8	teaspoons flour

Place the roast in a large, deep dish. Mix the vinegar, water, onions, lemon slices, cloves, bay leaves, peppercorns, salt, sugar and butter in a bowl. Pour over the roast. Marinate, covered, in the refrigerator for 3 days, turning roast occasionally. Remove the roast and pat dry; reserve the marinade. Brown the roast on all sides in hot oil in a heavy roasting pan. Strain the reserved marinade and pour over the roast. Bake, covered, at 350 degrees for 3 hours. Remove the roast to a carving rack and let stand for several minutes before slicing. Stir the flour into the pan juices. Simmer over low heat until thickened, stirring frequently. Serve with the roast.

Yield: 8 to 10 servings

Elizabeth Wolf, Society of the Danube Swabians

STEWED BEEF

1¼	pounds beef, cut into bite-sized pieces
	Flour
1	tablespoon oil
6	to 8 potatoes, sliced
1	carrot, sliced
2	onions, sliced
	Water or beef bouillon
½	cup sour cream
1	celery root, chopped
	Bay leaves

Pound the beef slightly to tenderize. Sprinkle with salt and pepper to taste and coat with flour. Fry in hot oil in a skillet until browned. Place in a heavy saucepan. Add the potatoes, carrot, onions and enough water to cover. Simmer, covered, over low heat for 30 to 45 minutes or until the vegetables are tender. Serve garnished with sour cream, celery and bay leaves.

Yield: 4 servings

Zoya Nikiforovich, Bielarusian Coordinating Committee of Chicago

EMPANADAS ECUATORIANAS *Ecuador*

MEAT TURNOVERS

MAIN DISHES

2   pounds ground beef

Salt and cumin to taste

2   pounds sifted flour
(about 6 cups)

1   cup lukewarm milk

1   teaspoon salt

1/2 cup butter or
margarine, at room
temperature

2   eggs, beaten

Oil for deep-frying

Brown the ground beef in a skillet, stirring until crumbly; drain. Season with salt and cumin and set aside. Combine the flour, milk and salt in a large bowl. Cut the butter into flour mixture. Add the eggs, stirring until a soft dough forms. Knead the dough until smooth and pliable. Shape the dough into a log 1 1/2 inches in diameter. Slice the log into 1 1/2-inch-thick portions. Roll out the dough into 1/8-inch-thick ovals. Spoon a small amount of the ground beef mixture over half of the oval. Fold the other half over to form a pocket. Press the edge with a fork to seal. Deep-fry in hot oil until golden brown, but do not fry more than 2 or 3 at a time and do not turn more than once. Drain on paper towels and serve hot.

Yield: 20 to 30 turnovers

*Maria T. Arellano and Ximena Bastidas,
Chicago Ecuadorean Lions Club*

THE TURNOVER IS A FAVORITE ITEM ON MANY MENUS. MAKING EMPANADAS IS SIMILAR TO THE PROCESS OF MAKING RAVIOLI, AND THEY SHOULD BE EATEN PIPING HOT. THESE CRISPY, DEEP-FRIED ECUADORIAN EMPANADAS MAY BE FILLED WITH GROUND BEEF, SHRIMP, OYSTERS, FISH, PORK, BEANS, SWEETS OR A SHREDDED WHITE CHEESE CALLED "QUESO FRESCO." TO SERVE AS APPETIZERS (CALLED "EMPANADITAS"), MAKE THE TURNOVERS SLIGHTLY SMALLER.

Main Dishes

In Ireland, Christmas is often a day of charity. Many families deliver platefuls of food to neighbors and friends who are unable to do their own cooking. Once this tradition is complete, the family then sits down to enjoy its own holiday dinner.

MINCE AND TATTIES *Scotland*

GROUND BEEF AND POTATOES

Scottish cooking is for the most part very basic—meat and potatoes main dishes.
One very popular dish is the following "Mince and Tatties."

1	onion, chopped
1	tablespoon bacon drippings
1	pound ground beef
	Salt and pepper to taste
1¼	cups beef stock
1	tablespoon rolled oats
2	bay leaves
	Cooked mashed potatoes

Sauté the onion in the bacon drippings in a heavy skillet until translucent but not browned. Remove from the heat. Add the ground beef, salt, pepper, beef stock, oats and bay leaves. Simmer over low heat for 45 minutes or until the ground beef is cooked through, stirring occasionally. Remove the bay leaves. Spoon onto serving plates and serve with mashed potatoes.

Yield: 4 servings
Nancy Strolle, Thistle & Heather Highland Dancers

Ireland

IRISH-AMERICAN MEAT PIE

2	tablespoons oil
1	large onion, thinly sliced
1	pound ground beef
1	pound ground pork
1	cup mashed potatoes
2	teaspoons ground allspice
1	teaspoon salt
¼	teaspoon pepper
1	recipe (2-crust) pie pastry
1	egg, beaten

Heat the oil in a skillet over medium heat. Sauté the onion until tender; remove and set aside. Add the ground beef and ground pork. Cook until the meat is crumbly and cooked through; drain well. Mix with the onion, potatoes, allspice, salt and pepper. Line a tart pan with half of the pastry. Spoon in the meat mixture. Top with the remaining pastry, pinching edge to seal. Cut slits in the pastry to allow steam to escape. Brush with the egg. Bake at 375 degrees for 30 to 35 minutes or until golden brown.

Yield: 6 to 8 servings
Mary Ellen McNicholas, Irish American Heritage Center

STUFFED NOODLES WITH AUNT ZINA'S SAUCE

MAIN DISHES

1   (16-ounce) package
      lasagna noodles

1   to 1¹/₂ pounds ricotta
      cheese

¹/₂   to ³/₄ cup grated
      Romano cheese

1¹/₂ teaspoons salt

³/₄   teaspoon coarsely
      ground pepper

¹/₂   teaspoon oregano

¹/₂   teaspoon parsley flakes

1   egg, slightly beaten
      Aunt Zina's Sauce

16   ounces mozzarella
      cheese, shredded

Cook the noodles using package directions; drain. While noodles are cooking, combine the ricotta and Romano cheeses, salt, pepper, oregano, parsley and egg in a medium bowl; mix well. Spread a small amount of the sauce over the bottom of a 9x13-inch baking pan. Alternate layers of the noodles, the cheese mixture, the mozzarella cheese and the sauce until all ingredients are used. Top with additional mozzarella cheese and Romano cheese. Bake at 350 degrees for 45 minutes or until bubbly.

Yield: 6 to 8 servings

Joey Filingeri

Pasta dates back in Italian history to as early as the 8th century. There are more than 100 shapes and sizes of pasta. It is a staple of the Italian diet, and Italian cooks have devised many ways to serve pasta: in sauce, in broth, or stuffed with meat or cheese. A typical holiday meal in Italy might include this version of lasagna, followed by Italian sausages or a roasted chicken, eggplant marinara and broccoli Siciliano, plus a vinaigrette salad, several fruits, and lots of wine.

AUNT ZINA'S SAUCE

1   medium onion

¹/₄   cup olive oil

3   to 4 cloves of garlic

8   ounces lean ground
      beef

1¹/₂ teaspoons oregano

1¹/₂ teaspoons basil

1¹/₂ teaspoons salt

1   teaspoon coarsely
      ground pepper

3   tablespoons sugar

2   (28-ounce) cans
      crushed tomatoes

³/₄   can water

Sauté the chopped onion in the oil in a skillet until golden brown. Add the minced garlic. Sauté for 1 minute or until lightly browned. Add the ground beef. Cook until crumbly and cooked through, stirring to break up. Stir in the oregano, basil, salt and pepper. Simmer for 1 minute. Add the sugar, tomatoes and water; reduce the heat. Simmer, partially covered, for 1 hour or until the sauce is reduced by about 1 cup, stirring occasionally. This sauce is better if prepared several hours ahead of time so the flavor can develop.

PASTICHIO *Greece*

GROUND BEEF AND MACARONI

*Pastichio is the Greek version of lasagna. This is served either as a main dish
or a side dish during holidays or any special occasion.*

1/2	cup butter or margarine
2 1/2	pounds ground beef
1	onion, chopped
2	tablespoons tomato paste
1	teaspoon cinnamon
	Salt and pepper to taste
1 1/2	cups water
1	pound macaroni
2 1/2	cups grated Kefalotiri or Romano cheese
8	eggs
	Crema

Melt the butter in a large skillet. Brown the
ground beef with the onion, stirring until the
ground beef is crumbly. Stir in the tomato
paste, cinnamon, salt, pepper and water.
Simmer for 45 minutes or until the liquid is
absorbed. Cook the macaroni using package
directions; drain well. Combine with the
cheese and ground beef mixture in a large
bowl. Beat 6 of the eggs and stir into the
mixture. Spoon into a buttered 11x15-inch
baking pan. Cover with the Crema. Beat the
remaining 2 eggs and pour evenly over the
Crema. Sprinkle with additional cinnamon.
Bake at 350 degrees for 45 minutes.

Yield: 6 to 8 servings

Joanne Sideris, Peiraikon Hellenic School

CREMA

1	quart milk
1/3	cup farina
1/2	cup butter or margarine
1	teaspoon salt
4	eggs, beaten
1/2	cup grated Kefalotiri cheese

Heat the milk in a heavy saucepan until
lukewarm. Add the farina, butter and salt.
Cook over medium heat for 10 minutes or
until the mixture thickens, stirring constantly.
Remove from the heat and let stand to cool
slightly. Add the eggs gradually, beating well.
Fold in the cheese. Spread over the Pastichio
mixture.

STUFFED EGGPLANT

MAIN DISHES

12	small, long eggplant or 6 medium eggplant
$1/4$	cup oil plus 2 tablespoons oil
1	pound ground beef
1	large onion, finely chopped
1	clove of garlic, minced
$1/4$	cup pine nuts
$1/4$	teaspoon cinnamon
$1/4$	teaspoon ground allspice
$1/4$	cup chopped parsley
	Salt and pepper to taste
1	cup tomato purée

Remove the stalks from the eggplant. Peel in $1/2$-inch intervals to create stripes. Heat $1/4$ cup oil in a large skillet. Brown the eggplant on all sides. Remove to a plate. Add the remaining 2 tablespoons oil, ground beef, onion, garlic, pine nuts, cinnamon, allspice, parsley, salt and pepper to the skillet. Cook over medium heat until the ground beef is browned and crumbly; remove from the heat. Cut a deep slit on one side of each eggplant. Spoon the ground beef mixture into the slit. Place the eggplant in a baking dish. Pour the tomato purée evenly over the top; season with additional salt and pepper. Bake at 375 degrees for 30 minutes, basting occasionally with pan juices. Add additional water if necessary.

Yield: 6 servings
Anita Kropp

Allspice, a combination of clove, cinnamon and nutmeg called "Bahar," flavors this eggplant dish. Served with rice, the taste is indescribable!

STUFFED PEPPERS

4	to 6 green bell peppers
$3/4$	pound ground beef
$1/2$	pound ground pork
$1/2$	onion, minced
$1/2$	teaspoon pepper
$1/2$	teaspoon salt
$1/2$	cup uncooked rice
1	egg, beaten
1	tablespoon butter
1	tablespoon flour
1	(8-ounce) can tomato paste

Slice off the tops of the peppers and remove the seeds and ribs; rinse. Combine the ground beef, ground pork, onion, pepper, salt, rice and egg in a bowl, mixing well. Spoon the filling into the green peppers. Place in a large saucepan and cover with water. Cook over low heat for 2 hours. Remove with a slotted spoon. Reserve remaining liquid from pan. Return peppers to the saucepan. Melt the butter in a small saucepan. Add the flour, stirring until browned. Stir in the tomato paste and enough water to make a smooth sauce. Season with a pinch of sugar and salt. Pour over the stuffed peppers. Simmer for 5 minutes longer.

Yield: 4 to 6 servings
Society of the Danube Swabians

MAIN DISHES

CABBAGE LEAVES, SPINACH, BEET LEAVES AND GRAPE LEAVES STUFFED WITH MEAT OR VEGETABLE FILLINGS ARE TRADITIONAL MAIN DISHES IN MANY COUNTRIES. THE FOLLOWING RECIPES FROM ROMANIA, SWEDEN, GERMANY AND THE UKRAINE DIFFER AS TO THE FILLING USED, BUT THE BASIC PREPARATION OF THE CABBAGE LEAVES IS STANDARD.

———

THE CABBAGE SHOULD BE RINSED WELL AND THE HARD CORE CUT OUT. PLACE THE CABBAGE IN A LARGE POT OF BOILING WATER. REDUCE THE HEAT TO LOW. SIMMER UNTIL THE OUTER LEAVES BEGIN TO WILT, ABOUT 1 MINUTE. REMOVE THE CABBAGE FROM THE WATER AND PEEL OFF THE TENDER OUTER LEAVES. RETURN THE CABBAGE TO THE WATER AND REPEAT THE PROCESS UNTIL A SUFFICIENT AMOUNT OF LEAVES HAVE BEEN REMOVED. SMALL OR DAMAGED LEAVES MAY BE USED TO LINE THE BAKING DISH. CUT OUT THE STEM PORTION AND GENTLY PAT THE LEAVES DRY. THEY ARE NOW READY TO BE FILLED WITH YOUR FAVORITE STUFFING.

Romania
STUFFED CABBAGE

2	heads of cabbage
2	onions, chopped
2	tablespoons olive oil
2	tablespoons rice
3/4	pound ground beef
3/4	pound ground pork
1/2	pound ground smoked ham
2	teaspoons chopped dillweed
	Salt and pepper to taste
2	tablespoons tomato juice
1	jar sauerkraut, drained
10	tomatoes
1	cup water

Prepare the cabbage as directed at left. Sauté the onions in olive oil in a large skillet until golden brown. Add the rice. Simmer for 5 minutes longer. Add 2 tablespoons of water to the skillet. Simmer, covered, over medium-high heat for 15 minutes or until the rice is softened. Set aside to cool. Mix with the next 7 ingredients in a large bowl. Spoon the mixture onto each cabbage leaf, folding sides and ends to enclose the filling. Layer 1/3 of the sauerkraut, half of the tomatoes and half of the cabbage rolls in a Dutch oven. Repeat the layers, ending with the sauerkraut. Pour in 1 cup of water. Simmer, covered, over low heat for 1 hour, shaking the Dutch oven occasionally to prevent sticking. Remove from the heat. Add additional tomato juice, and season with salt and pepper. Bake, covered, at 400 degrees for 30 minutes. Serve with polenta and sour cream.

Yield: 10 to 12 servings
The Romanian Christmas Group Holy Nativity

KÅLDOLMAR *Sweden*
STUFFED CABBAGE

1	large head of cabbage
1	pound each ground beef and ground pork
1	onion, chopped
1	cup cooked rice
2	teaspoons salt
1/4	teaspoon each pepper and ground allspice
	Butter for frying
	Brown sugar or dark corn syrup

Prepare the cabbage leaves as directed at left. Mix the ground beef, ground pork, onion, rice, salt, pepper and allspice in a bowl. Spoon the filling into the cabbage leaves, folding to enclose. Brush the ends with egg white or secure with a wooden pick. Brown the rolls in butter in a skillet. Transfer to a baking dish. Sprinkle with brown sugar or drizzle with corn syrup. Bake at 325 degrees for 1 hour.

Yield: 8 servings
Lillian Wennlund, Linnea South Suburban Swedish Women's Club

SARMA *Germany*
STUFFED CABBAGE OR "PIGS IN THE BLANKET"

1	head of cabbage
3/4	pound each ground beef and pork
2	tablespoons salt
1	teaspoon pepper
1	cup uncooked rice
1	egg, beaten
1	large onion, minced
1	pound sauerkraut
1	bay leaf

Prepare the cabbage leaves as directed on page 54. Mix the next 7 ingredients in a bowl. Spoon a small amount of the mixture onto each cabbage leaf. Line the bottom of a large saucepan with smaller cabbage leaves. Alternate layers of sauerkraut and cabbage rolls, packing the rolls tightly. Cover 2/3 with water. Add the bay leaf. Simmer, covered, over low heat for 2 hours or until tender and cooked through. Remove the bay leaf before serving.

Yield: 8 servings
Society of the Danube Swabians

UKRAINIANS CELEBRATE THE CHRISTMAS SEASON FROM CHRISTMAS EVE (JANUARY 6) TO THE FEAST OF JORDAN (JANUARY 19). THE FAMILY FASTS ALL DAY AND BREAKS THE FAST WITH THE CHRISTMAS EVE SUPPER (SVIATA VECHERA).

HOLUBTSI *Ukraine*
MUSHROOM-STUFFED CABBAGE ROLLS

1	large head of cabbage
2	ounces dried mushrooms
3	cups water
1	cup chopped onion
1	cup vegetable oil
2	cups rice
	Salt and pepper to taste
2	cups tomato juice

Prepare the cabbage leaves as directed on page 54. Simmer the mushrooms with water in a saucepan for 1 hour. Strain the mushroom stock and reserve. Chop the mushrooms and set aside. Sauté the onion in a skillet with 1/2 cup of the oil. Cook the rice in the reserved mushroom stock until slightly tender. Add the mushrooms and half of the sautéed onion. Season with salt and pepper. Spoon 1 tablespoon of the mixture onto the cabbage leaves. Fold up the sides and roll up loosely. Layer the cabbage rolls in a large baking dish. Pour the tomato juice evenly over the rolls. Sprinkle with the remaining oil and onion. Bake, covered, at 350 degrees for 1 hour. Serve with sour cream or mushroom sauce.

Yield: 8 servings
Ukrainian National Women's League,
Branch 22, in Chicago

MAIN DISHES

CHARSHU MAY BE SERVED AS AN APPETIZER OR AS A MAIN DISH WITH YANG CHOW FRIED RICE (PAGE 100). HAVE YOUR BUTCHER CUT THROUGH THE HEAVY BONE ALONG THE BOTTOM OF THE RIBS BEFORE BEGINNING PREPARATION.

CHARSHU *China*

CHINESE BARBECUED PORK

1	whole section center-cut pork ribs
2	cups soy sauce
2	cups sugar
1/2	cup oil
1/4	cup dry red or white wine
	Minced garlic to taste
	MSG to taste

Prepare the ribs by removing all fat and cutting away the ribs. Slice the meat into strips and place in a large shallow baking dish. Mix the soy sauce, sugar, oil, wine, garlic and MSG in a small bowl. Pour evenly over the meat. Marinate for 8 to 10 hours in the refrigerator. Bake in a 300-degree oven for 2 to 3 hours or until the pork is tender and cooked through, brushing with pan juices from time to time. Cool thoroughly before slicing into thin strips to serve.

Yield: 6 to 8 servings
Taye Yamaguchi

Hawaii

OVEN KALUA PIG

Ingredients for a successful Hawaiian feast are hospitality, informality, friendliness, flowers, good food, music and dancing.

2	tablespoons Hawaiian salt
1/4	cup soy sauce
1	teaspoon Worcestershire sauce
2	cloves of garlic, crushed
1	piece of fresh ginger, crushed
1	tablespoon liquid smoke
1	(4- to 5-pound) pork roast
	Ti or banana leaves

Combine the salt, soy sauce, Worcestershire sauce, garlic, ginger and liquid smoke in a small bowl, mixing well. Place the roast on several ti or banana leaves. Rub with the prepared sauce and let stand for 1 hour. Fold the leaves over to enclose the roast and place in a baking pan. Bake at 325 degrees for 4 to 5 hours or until the roast is cooked through. Unwrap and discard the leaves. Let stand to cool slightly. Shred the meat and place on a serving platter.

Yield: 6 to 8 servings
Lynette "Lineaka" Troha, Stars of the South Pacific

PORK CURRY

2 pounds pork roast or pork round

12 small dried red chiles

1¹/₂ teaspoons cumin seeds

1¹/₂ tablespoons coriander seeds

¹/₄ teaspoon mustard seeds

6 peppercorns

1 teaspoon khus khus (poppy seeds)

¹/₂ teaspoon saunf (fennel seeds)

5 cloves

2 cardamom pods

1 (2-inch) cinnamon stick

1 medium onion, chopped

¹/₂ teaspoon turmeric

¹/₄ cup vinegar

1 tablespoon salt

1 (1-inch) piece of ginger, chopped

8 cloves of garlic, chopped

3 medium green chiles, sliced

1 tomato, chopped

1 medium tamarind, soaked

3 bay leaves

2 large onions, cut into 2-inch slices

Slice the pork roast into 2-inch pieces. Rinse and set aside. Fry in a nonstick skillet the red chiles, cumin seeds, coriander seeds, mustard seeds, peppercorns, poppy seeds, fennel seeds, cloves, cardamom pods, cinnamon, chopped onion and turmeric, one ingredient at a time. Place the cooled spices and onion in a blender container with the vinegar. Process until a smooth, thick paste forms, adding a small amount of water for desired consistency. Stir in the salt. Rub the ground spices into the pork slices. Marinate for 15 minutes or longer. Place the pork in a large kettle. Add the ginger, garlic, green chiles and tomato. Strain the tamarind pulp and add the liquid and the bay leaves to the pork mixture. Simmer over low heat for 1 hour. Add the sliced onions. Simmer for 30 minutes longer or until the pork is tender. Remove the bay leaves. Serve with boiled rice or sannas, which are dumplings made of rice, or dals (lentil purée).

Yield: 8 servings

Jacintha B. Martis, India Catholic Association of America

THIS RECIPE IS FROM MANGALORE, A PORT TOWN SOUTH OF GOA ON THE WEST COAST OF INDIA. PORK CURRY IS A TRADITIONAL DISH DURING MAJOR FESTIVALS, SUCH AS CHRISTMAS, BUT IT ALSO IS SERVED DURING OTHER IMPORTANT OCCASIONS WHEN THE COMMUNITY USES A WHOLE PIG AND SHARES THE MEAT WITH ALL THE FAMILIES. A PROPERLY PREPARED INDIAN CURRY HAS A VERY SUBTLE FLAVOR, WHICH IS ENHANCED BY FRYING THE SPICES INDIVIDUALLY TO BRING OUT THEIR ESSENCE. THE DEGREE OF "HOTNESS" OR SPICINESS IS DETERMINED BY THE AMOUNT OF CHILES AND PEPPERS USED IN THE DISH. THE TAMARIND, AN ESSENTIAL INGREDIENT IN THIS RECIPE, IS ALSO CALLED THE INDIAN DATE. IF YOU ARE UNABLE TO FIND A WHOLE TAMARIND, THE PULP IN CONCENTRATE IS USUALLY AVAILABLE IN INDIAN GROCERIES.

Main Dishes

A very different version of a pork dish comes to us from Germany. This hearty dish is served with cottage cheese, sauerkraut, pickled beets and good German rye bread. Dwight O. Von Ahnen from the German-American Children's Chorus prepares Smoked Butt Tokana (Pork and Potato Stew) as follows: Cube 3 1/2 pounds smoked pork butt roast. Place in a 6-quart saucepan with 1 chopped medium yellow onion and 6 cubed peeled potatoes. Sprinkle with pepper and paprika to taste. Pour in 1 cup water. Cook, covered, over medium heat for 30 to 40 minutes or until the pork is cooked through and the potatoes are tender. This recipe yields 6 servings.

Mørbrad med Svedsker og Æbler *Denmark*
Pork Loin Stuffed with Prunes and Apple

Ham, pork and bacon are widely used in Denmark, and Danish chefs have created many specialties using these meats combined with fruits, as in the following recipe.

12	medium pitted prunes
1	large tart apple
1	teaspoon lemon juice
1	(4 1/2- to 5-pound) boneless center-cut pork loin
	Salt and freshly ground pepper to taste
3	tablespoons butter
3	tablespoons vegetable oil
3/4	cup dry white wine
3/4	cup heavy cream
1	tablespoon red currant jelly

Place the prunes in a saucepan and cover with water. Bring to a boil; remove from the heat. Soak the prunes for 30 minutes. Drain and pat dry with paper towels. Peel and core the apple and cut into 1-inch cubes. Sprinkle with lemon juice to prevent discoloration. Cut a deep slit through the center of pork loin to within 1 inch of the bottom and up to 1/2 inch from each end. Sprinkle with salt and pepper. Fill the pocket with the prunes and apple. Sew up the opening with strong kitchen thread or use skewers; tie at 1-inch intervals to retain the shape while cooking. Preheat the oven to 350 degrees. Melt the butter with the oil in a Dutch oven over moderate heat on the stove. Add the pork loin and brown it on all sides for about 20 minutes, turning frequently. Remove loin to heated platter. Skim all the fat from the pan. Pour in the wine and cream, whisking briskly. Return loin to Dutch oven. Heat until the mixture begins to simmer. Bake, covered, in the center of the oven for 1 1/2 hours or until the pork is cooked through. Remove to a heated platter. Skim any fat from the pan. Bring the sauce to a boil on the stove. Cook until the liquid is reduced to 1 cup. Stir in the jelly; reduce the heat. Simmer until the sauce is smooth, stirring constantly. Season to taste. Pour into a serving dish. Slice the pork loin into 1-inch slices and arrange on serving plates.

Yield: 6 to 8 servings

Erma Prewett, Danish Sisterhood Society, Olga Lodge 177

SAUTÉED PORK, SAUSAGE, SHRIMP AND RICE NOODLES

2	packages Oriental rice noodles
1/4	cup dried mushrooms
1	cup pork strips
3	large cloves of garlic, crushed
1/2	cup sliced onion
2	tablespoons oil
1/2	cup shelled shrimp
1/4	cup thinly sliced Chinese sausage
1/2	cup cabbage strips
1/2	cup carrot strips
1/4	cup chopped celery
1/2	cup soy sauce

Soak the noodles in water for 10 to 15 minutes or until slightly softened; drain and set aside. Soak the mushrooms in water to soften. Cut into strips and set aside. Sauté the pork strips, garlic and onion in the oil in a large skillet until the pork begins to lose its pinkness. Cut the shrimp into halves lengthwise. Add the shrimp, sausage and mushrooms. Sauté until the shrimp turn pink. Add the cabbage, carrot, and celery. Stir-fry until the vegetables are tender-crisp. Add the noodles, soy sauce, salt, pepper and MSG to taste. Stir-fry until the noodles are tender. Serve garnished with lemon juice.

Yield: 6 servings

Rosemary Mittenthal, Sampaguita Singers of Chicago, Inc.

THESE RECIPES FROM THE PHILIPPINES REFLECT THE INFLUENCE OF THE TWO COUNTRIES THAT INHABITED THESE ISLANDS. THE PANCIT HAS A CHINESE FLAVOR, WHILE THE ADOBO HAS A SPANISH FLAVOR. BOTH DISHES ARE PREPARED AND COOKED IN AS MANY DIFFERENT WAYS AS THERE ARE REGIONS IN THE PHILIPPINES.

PANCIT MAY BE SERVED ALONE FOR A LIGHT MEAL OR WITH OTHER MAIN DISHES FOR A HEAVY MEAL. IN THE PHILIPPINES, LUNCH AND SUPPER ARE CONSIDERED HEAVY MEALS.

STEWED PORK IN SOY SAUCE AND VINEGAR

2	pounds country-style pork ribs
1/2	cup vinegar
1/2	cup soy sauce
5	large cloves of garlic, crushed
20	black peppercorns
1	tablespoon salt
2	to 3 bay leaves

Remove the meat from the bones and cut into cubes. Place in a large saucepan. Combine the vinegar, soy sauce, garlic, peppercorns and salt in a small bowl. Pour over the meat and cover. Stew over low heat until tender. Add the bay leaves. Stew for 5 minutes longer. Serve with steamed vegetables and boiled white rice. May substitute 2 teaspoons garlic powder for the cloves of garlic and 1 teaspoon ground pepper for the peppercorns.

Yield: 6 servings

Rosemary Mittenthal, Sampaguita Singers of Chicago, Inc.

ADOBO IS OFTEN SERVED AT PARTIES AND FESTIVALS. FOR VARIETY, YOU MAY SUBSTITUTE 3 POUNDS OF CHICKEN OR 3 POUNDS OF BEEF RIBS FOR THE PORK RIBS, OR YOU MAY COMBINE ALL THREE USING 1 POUND OF EACH MEAT.

Main Dishes

In Canada, the pork in these minced pies is often replaced with beef, venison, moose or caribou, or a combination of these meats. The pies may be partially baked and frozen for later use. Microwaving is not recommended because the pastry does not turn out well.

TOURTIÈRE *Canada*

MINCED PORK PIES

2	large onions, chopped
1¹/₂	cups water
¹/₆	teaspoon ground cloves
¹/₆	teaspoon cinnamon
¹/₂	teaspoon black pepper
1	teaspoon salt
	Cayenne pepper, celery salt and onion salt to taste
3	pounds lean pork, minced
3	to 4 slices white bread, cubed
	Flour
	Double recipe (2-crust) pie pastry

Sauté the onions in a large nonstick skillet until tender. Add the water, cloves, cinnamon, black pepper, salt, cayenne pepper, celery salt and onion salt, stirring well. Add the pork. Simmer over medium heat for 30 minutes, stirring often. Remove from the heat. Skim off fat. Add the bread cubes to soak up some of the broth. Stir in enough flour to thicken the sauce. Let stand to cool. Line two deep-dish pie plates with half of the pastry. Spoon in the pork mixture. Top with the remaining pie pastry, cutting slits to ventilate. Bake in a preheated 425-degree oven for 10 minutes. Reduce oven temperature to 350 degrees and bake for 35 minutes or until top is golden brown.

Yield: 10 to 12 servings
The Canadian Women's Club of Chicago

JAMBON CABANE À SUCRE *Canada*

HAM STEAKS IN MAPLE SYRUP

Justly famous for its maple syrup, a Canadian menu would not be complete without a dish featuring this delectable ingredient.

2	(1¹/₂-inch) thick ham steaks
2	teaspoons dry mustard
2	tablespoons cider vinegar
¹/₂	cup maple syrup

Remove the fat and rind from the ham steaks. Combine the mustard, vinegar and maple syrup in a small bowl. Brush over both sides of the ham steaks. Place in a baking pan and drizzle with the remaining syrup mixture. Bake at 350 degrees for 30 minutes.

Yield: 2 to 4 servings
The Canadian Women's Club of Chicago

Homemade Sausage with Sauerkraut

Sausage-making time is traditionally associated with holidays and parties.

10   pounds fresh pork shoulder

2   pounds smoked pork butt

1   large onion, chopped

3   cloves of garlic, chopped

1/4   cup salt

1   tablespoon pepper

1   tablespoon allspice

4   cups water

    Sausage casings

Grind the pork coarsely in a meat grinder. Sauté the onion and garlic in a nonstick skillet until tender. Combine with the ground pork, salt, pepper and allspice in a large bowl. Mix by hand, adding water for desired consistency. Wash the sausage casings and attach to a sausage stuffer, knotting one end of the casing. Stuff with the meat mixture, knotting the end when of desired length. Store in the refrigerator until ready to use. Cook the sausage in boiling water for 1 hour. Drain well and serve with sauerkraut.

Yield: 40 to 50 sausages
Bernice Kasarski

In Lithuania, family members gather together for the Christmas Eve Dinner called Kucios. Everyone sits at the dinner table as soon as the first star appears in the sky. If a family member has died that year, an empty place is left at the table.

SAUERKRAUT

1   small head cabbage, chopped

1   (28-ounce) can sauerkraut

8   ounces bacon, chopped

1   medium onion, chopped

    Salt to taste

1   teaspoon caraway seeds

Cook the cabbage in simmering water in a large saucepan for 3 to 5 minutes or until it begins to wilt; drain. Add the sauerkraut. Simmer gently for 5 to 10 minutes. Sauté the bacon and onion until lightly browned. Stir into the sauerkraut mixture. Add salt and caraway seeds. Simmer until heated through. Serve with homemade sausage.

Yield: 12 to 15 servings

Main Dishes

Sausage making is a family affair for the Swedes, and since this recipe makes a lot, it's good to share with friends and family who pitch in to peel the potatoes. For best results, have the butcher grind the meat together twice. Place the sausages in freezer bags and freeze immediately until ready to use, as the potatoes will discolor.

Sweden

SWEDISH POTATO SAUSAGE WITH ROTMOS

5	pounds potatoes, peeled, grated
2¹/₂	pounds ground beef
2¹/₂	pounds ground pork
3	tablespoons (heaping) salt
1¹/₂	tablespoons (heaping) pepper
1	tablespoon (heaping) crushed allspice
3	medium yellow onions, finely chopped
1	pound sausage casings
1	bay leaf
	Peppercorns

Combine the potatoes, ground beef, ground pork, salt, pepper, allspice and onions in a large bowl. Knead well to mix. Fill the sausage casings with the mixture, tying off the ends. Place the sausages in an 18-inch pan filled with water to cover. Prick the casings with a fork to prevent cracking while cooking. Add a bay leaf and a few peppercorns. Boil for 1 to 1¹/₂ hours. Drain and cool slightly. Cut the sausage into 3-inch lengths. Serve with mustard and Rotmos.

Yield: 30 to 40 sausages

Jean Svedberg, Linnea South Suburban Swedish Women's Club

ROTMOS

1¹/₂	pounds yellow turnips
1	pound potatoes
	Butter
	Cream

Peel the turnips and potatoes and cut into cubes. Place in a large saucepan with water to cover. Boil until tender; drain well. Mash with butter and cream. Beat with electric mixer until fluffy.

Yield: 12 to 14 servings

SAUSAGE WITH POTATOES AND KALE

1   pound fresh or frozen kale

2   to 3 pounds potatoes, peeled

1¹/₂   pounds smoked sausage

3   to 4 cups water

¹/₄   cup butter

1   teaspoon salt

Remove the large veins from the kale. Place in a saucepan with a small amount of water. Simmer for 10 minutes. Drain well, squeezing out excess water. Chop finely. Layer the potatoes, kale and sausage in a 3-quart saucepan. Add water. Simmer over low heat for 1 to 1¹/₂ hours. Remove the sausage and set aside. Drain off the excess water. Add the butter and salt. Mash the potatoes and kale together. Spoon into the center of a serving plate. Cut the sausages into thick slices and arrange around or on top of the potato mixture.

Yield: 6 servings

Cindy Sluis, Chicago Museum Committee

Greece

ROAST LEG OF LAMB

1   (6- to 7-pound) leg of lamb

¹/₄   cup melted butter

¹/₄   cup olive oil

3   cloves of garlic, cut into slivers

2   teaspoons salt

1   teaspoon pepper

2   teaspoons oregano

    Juice of 1 lemon

1   cup water

Rinse the leg of lamb and pat dry. Place on a rack in a roasting pan. Make several slits in the lamb. Mix the butter and olive oil in a small bowl. Dip the garlic slivers in the mixture. Insert the garlic into the slits in the lamb. Sprinkle with a mixture of the salt, pepper and oregano. Rub the remaining butter mixture over the surface of the lamb. Drizzle with the lemon juice. Roast, tightly covered, at 325 degrees for 3 hours. Add water during roasting and baste with pan drippings. Small onions or other vegetables may be added to the roasting pan halfway through the cooking time.

Yield: 10 servings

Dina Roiniotis, Peiraikon Hellenic School

MAIN DISHES

IN THE NORTHERN PART OF HOLLAND, DISHES COMBINING MEAT AND VEGETABLES SUCH AS SAUERKRAUT, KALE OR WHITE BEANS (KNOWN GENERICALLY AS "HUTSPOTS") ARE VERY COMMON. THEY ARE BOTH HEALTHY AND ECONOMICAL, AND ARE ESPECIALLY GOOD ON A COLD WINTER'S EVENING. INSTEAD OF KALE, YOU MAY SUBSTITUTE CARROTS OR WHITE CABBAGE. APPLESAUCE IS AN EXCELLENT ACCOMPANIMENT FOR BOERENKOOL.

IN GREECE, LAMB IS A STAPLE MEAT AND IS TRADITIONALLY SERVED ON SUNDAYS AND DURING ALL CELEBRATIONS, ESPECIALLY EASTER.

MAIN DISHES

KOFTE KI BIRYANI *India*
SAVORY SPICED LAMB WITH RICE

*To enhance the flavor and color of rice, Indian cooks often
add a pinch of turmeric or saffron.*

4	cups chopped onions
3	cloves of garlic, chopped
2	tablespoons chopped gingerroot
1	teaspoon roasted cumin seeds
1	teaspoon coriander seeds
1	green bell pepper, chopped
1/4	cup lemon juice
8	ounces plain yogurt
1/2	cup water
1	teaspoon paprika
2	teaspoons salt
1	(2-pound) leg of lamb, cut into cubes
1/4	cup butter
2	cups basmati rice
4	teaspoons milk
1	teaspoon turmeric
1/4	cup cashews and blanched almonds
8	whole cardamom pods, crushed
4	sticks of cinnamon
6	bay leaves

Process half of the onions with the garlic, gingerroot, cumin, coriander and green pepper in a blender until finely ground. Mix with lemon juice, yogurt, water, paprika and 1 teaspoon of the salt in a shallow bowl. Add the lamb cubes. Marinate in the refrigerator for 8 to 10 hours. Melt half of the butter in a skillet. Add the marinated lamb. Cook, covered, over low heat for 20 minutes; remove the cover. Simmer until the pan drippings evaporate. Bring 6 cups of water and the remaining teaspoon salt to a boil in a medium saucepan. Add the rice. Cook for 5 minutes; drain. Brown the remaining 2 cups onions in the remaining butter in a skillet. Mix the milk and turmeric in a small bowl. Layer the lamb, rice, onions, mixed nuts, cardamom, cinnamon and bay leaves in a large baking pan. Drizzle with the milk mixture and any remaining butter. Cover tightly with foil. Bake at 325 degrees for 30 minutes. Garnish with raisins, nuts and cilantro and serve with yogurt salad.

Yield: 4 servings

Rosemary Thalanany, India Catholic Association of America

BUFTAKE *Egypt*
BREADED MINT-FLAVORED VEAL CUTLETS

6   to 8 veal cutlets
1   medium onion, cut
     into rings
    Salt and pepper to taste
2   tablespoons dried mint
1   to 2 eggs, beaten
    Bread crumbs
    Oil for frying

Pound the veal cutlets to $1/4$-inch thickness. Sprinkle the onion rings with salt, pepper and mint. Alternate layers of veal and onion in a shallow dish. Refrigerate, covered, for 1 hour. Remove the cutlets from the dish. Dip in the egg and coat with bread crumbs. Sauté in hot oil in a skillet until golden brown on each side. Serve garnished with parsley or potato chips.

Yield: 6 to 8 servings
Mary N. Khair, St. Mark's Coptic Church

MAIN DISHES

CHILDREN AND ADULTS
LOVE THIS RECIPE FOR
BUFTAKE. IT IS FREQUENTLY
PREPARED TO SERVE
TO GUESTS.

———

TO PREPARE CAPER SAUCE FOR
THE BREADED VEAL CUTLETS,
MELT 3 TABLESPOONS
BUTTER IN A SAUCEPAN.
ADD 3 TABLESPOONS FLOUR,
$3/4$ TEASPOON SALT AND
PAPRIKA TO TASTE. STIR UNTIL
SMOOTH. ADD 2 CUPS MILK
GRADUALLY, STIRRING
CONSTANTLY. BRING THE
MIXTURE TO A BOIL; REDUCE
HEAT. ADD 1 TABLESPOON
DRAINED CAPERS AND
2 TABLESPOONS LEMON
JUICE. SIMMER GENTLY
FOR 1 MINUTE.

WIENER SCHNITZEL *Germany*
BREADED VEAL CUTLETS IN CAPER SAUCE

2   pounds veal cutlets
$3/4$ cup fresh lemon juice
    Salt and pepper to taste
$1/2$ cup flour
2   eggs, beaten
1   cup bread crumbs
$1^1/2$ cups shortening
    Caper Sauce (at right)

Pound the cutlets to $1/4$-inch thickness. Marinate in the lemon juice in a shallow dish for 1 hour. Drain and pat dry. Sprinkle with salt and pepper. Dust with the flour, dip in the beaten eggs and coat with bread crumbs. Refrigerate for 20 minutes to set the breading. Heat the shortening in a heavy skillet. Add the cutlets. Cook over medium heat for 5 minutes on each side or until golden brown. Drizzle with the Caper Sauce.

Yield: 4 to 6 servings
Society of the Danube Swabians

MAIN DISHES

THIS IS A SPECIALTY
FROM ZURICH IN CENTRAL
SWITZERLAND AND IS
GENERALLY SERVED WITH
ROESTI, OR HASH BROWNS,
WHICH ARE A VERY POPULAR
SIDE DISH SIMILAR TO POTATO
PANCAKES OR LATKES.

ZUERCHER GESCHNETZELTES MIT ROESTI *Switzerland*

VEAL IN MUSHROOM GRAVY WITH HASH BROWN POTATOES

2¹/₂   pounds veal

1   teaspoon salt

    Freshly ground pepper to taste

2   tablespoons flour

    Oil for frying

2   tablespoons butter or margarine

1   onion, chopped

1   pound mushrooms, sliced

2   teaspoons lemon juice

1   cup white wine

1   cup clear beef broth

2   cups whipping cream

2   tablespoons cornstarch

    Roesti

Cut the veal into bite-sized pieces. Sprinkle with a mixture of salt, pepper and flour. Heat the oil in a large heavy skillet. Fry the veal briefly until just golden brown. Place in an ovenproof dish and keep warm in a 140-degree oven. Melt the butter over medium-low heat in a saucepan. Add the onion. Steam over low heat until tender but not browned. Add the mushrooms and the lemon juice. Steam until the mushrooms are tender. Add the wine. Bring to a boil. Cook until the liquid is reduced by half. Combine the beef broth, cream and cornstarch in a bowl, mixing well. Pour gradually into the sauce. Simmer until just heated through, stirring frequently. Stir in the veal. Season with salt and pepper. Spoon into a serving dish and garnish with parsley. Serve with Roesti.

Yield: 8 servings
Swiss Club of Chicago

ROESTI

5   pounds of potatoes, peeled

    Salt and pepper to taste

5   tablespoons butter

Cook the potatoes in boiling salted water in a large saucepan until tender. Drain and cool. Grate the potatoes coarsely and season with salt and pepper. Melt the butter in a large nonstick skillet. Add the potatoes. Cook over low heat, stirring occasionally. Form potatoes into a pie; cover and cook on low heat until golden brown. Turn gently. Cook for 5 to 6 minutes or until browned. Serve on a preheated plate.

Yield: 8 servings

China

CHICKEN WITH SNOW PEAS

8 ounces boneless
   chicken breast

¹/₂ egg white

1 teaspoon cornstarch

1 teaspoon white wine

1 teaspoon sesame oil

1 piece ginger

1 clove of garlic

1 cup oil

12 snow pea pods,
   trimmed

¹/₂ cup chicken stock

1 teaspoon (scant) salt

Rinse the chicken and pat dry. Slice thinly. Coat with a mixture of the egg white, cornstarch, wine and sesame oil. Fry the ginger and garlic in the oil in a skillet for 1 minute. Remove the garlic and ginger and discard. Stir-fry the chicken for 1 minute; remove to a warmed plate. Drain off all but 2 tablespoons oil from the skillet. Trim the ends from the snow peas. Stir-fry snow pea pods for 1 minute. Pour in the chicken stock. Cook for 1 minute longer. Add the chicken and salt. Heat for 1 minute longer.

Yield: 6 servings

Ginger Cheung, Chinese American Civic Council

KARAAGE CHICKEN *Japan*

GINGERED CHICKEN

1¹/₂ pounds boneless
   chicken breast

3 tablespoons soy sauce

2 tablespoons sake

1 tablespoon mirin

1 teaspoon sugar

1 tablespoon freshly
   grated ginger

1 cup cornstarch

3 cups oil

Rinse the chicken and pat dry. Cut into bite-sized pieces. Combine the soy sauce, sake, mirin, sugar and ginger in a shallow bowl. Add the chicken. Marinate for 30 minutes, turning occasionally. Remove the chicken and drain well. Coat with cornstarch. Heat the oil in a wok or deep fryer. Fry the chicken until golden brown, turning occasionally. Fry only 4 to 5 pieces at a time to keep the temperature of the oil constant.

Yield: 4 servings

Alice Nakashima

MAIN DISHES

CHICKEN IS A VERY POPULAR ITEM ON A CHINESE MENU AND IT IS COMMON TO SERVE TWO OR THREE DIFFERENT CHICKEN DISHES FOR A FEAST. THIS IS A "HOT WINE DISH" FROM THE PEKING REGION. AT A DINNER PARTY, NORMALLY FOUR HOT WINE DISHES ARE SERVED, FOLLOWED BY FOUR COLD WINE DISHES.

———

THIS CHICKEN DISH FROM JAPAN CAN BE SERVED AS AN APPETIZER OR A MAIN DISH AND IS A FAVORITE AT ANY TIME OF THE YEAR. THE SAKE AND MIRIN ARE BOTH MADE OF FERMENTED RICE, BUT THE MIRIN IS SLIGHTLY SWEETER THAN SAKE. RICE WINE IS FREQUENTLY USED IN JAPANESE COOKING TO ADD FLAVOR AND SWEETNESS.

Israel

CHICKEN CURRY

This is one of the principal dishes of the Cochin Jews of India, that has now been incorporated into Israeli cuisine.

1	(2-pound) chicken
1	tablespoon oil
¹/₂	cup water
5	large onions, chopped
2	cloves of garlic, minced
4	large tomatoes, chopped
1	cup chopped parsley
2	apples, peeled, chopped
2	tablespoons sugar
1	teaspoon ground ginger
1	tablespoon curry powder
1¹/₂	cups flour
3	cups clear broth or coconut milk
2	tablespoons grated coconut

Rinse the chicken and pat dry. Cut into serving portions. Fry in oil in a skillet until lightly browned. Add the water. Simmer for 20 minutes or until the chicken is tender. Remove the chicken to a warm plate. Add the onions, garlic, tomatoes, parsley and apples. Sauté over medium heat. Stir in the sugar, ginger and curry powder. Sprinkle with the flour. Stir in the broth. Add the coconut and the chicken pieces. Sauté over medium heat for 10 minutes longer. Serve hot with rice.

Yield: 4 servings

Embassy of Israel and Consulate General of Israel to the Midwest

PILECI PAPRIKAS *Croatia*
CHICKEN PAPRIKASH

1	(3-pound) chicken
2	onions, chopped
1/4	cup shortening
3	to 4 tablespoons water
1	teaspoon paprika
2	firm tomatoes, peeled, sliced
2	green bell peppers, seeded, sliced
3	tablespoons sour cream
1/2	teaspoon cayenne pepper

Rinse the chicken and pat dry. Cut into serving pieces. Sauté the onions in the shortening in a large heavy skillet until tender. Add 3 to 4 tablespoons water. Simmer until the water evaporates. Place the chicken over the onions. Sprinkle with paprika. Add enough water to cover. Simmer, covered, until the chicken is tender, stirring occasionally and adding water as needed. Add the tomatoes and green peppers. Simmer until the peppers are tender and the chicken is cooked through. Stir in the sour cream just before serving. Sprinkle with cayenne pepper.

Yield: 4 servings

Josephine Crame, Sacred Heart Croatian School, Kolo and Tambura Group

STCHU CHICKEN *Belize*
STEWED CHICKEN

This dish is served on Sundays and holidays in Belize.

1	(2-pound) chicken
1/4	cup vinegar
	Salt and pepper to taste
	Oregano, parsley, garlic and poultry seasoning to taste
1/2	cup oil
1	large onion, chopped
1	green bell pepper, chopped
2	ribs celery, chopped
1	(12-ounce) can tomato sauce or canned tomatoes

Rinse the chicken and pat dry. Cut into serving pieces. Combine the vinegar, salt, pepper, oregano, parsley, garlic and poultry seasoning in a shallow bowl. Add the chicken. Marinate in the refrigerator for 1 to 2 hours, turning occasionally to coat. Heat the oil in a large skillet. Drain the chicken, reserving the marinade. Sauté in the hot oil until browned on all sides. Add the onion, green pepper, celery, tomato sauce and reserved marinade. Simmer for 20 minutes or until the chicken is tender. Serve over plain rice or rice and beans.

Yield: 4 servings

Birdy Haggerty-Francis, Belizean Cultural Association

MAIN DISHES

IT IS STILL BELIEVED IN SOME SECTIONS OF CROATIA THAT ON CHRISTMAS EVE, ANGELS PASS OVER SPRINGS OF WATER, TOUCHING THEM WITH THEIR WINGS AND PURIFYING THEM. THE BLESSED WATER IS THEN USED IN MANY RECIPES AND A FLASK IS KEPT IN THE HOME TO USE THROUGHOUT THE YEAR.

MAIN DISHES

POULET AU YASSA *Senegal*

CHICKEN WITH LIMES

This dish is a specialty in the south of Senegal. Other meat or fish may be substituted for the chicken.

1   (3-pound) chicken
3   large onions, finely chopped
1   green bell pepper, minced
2   to 3 cloves of garlic, minced
    Salt and pepper to taste
    Juice of 3 limes
1/4   cup peanut oil
1   cup water
4   cups cooked rice

Rinse the chicken and pat dry. Cut into serving pieces. Combine the onions, green pepper, garlic, salt, pepper, lime juice and peanut oil in a shallow bowl. Add the chicken. Marinate for 2 to 3 hours in the refrigerator, turning occasionally to coat. Remove and drain the chicken, reserving the marinade. Sauté the chicken in a large nonstick skillet until browned and cooked through. Remove to a warm plate. Pour the reserved marinade into the skillet. Cook over medium heat until the onion is translucent. Add the chicken and water. Simmer for 30 minutes. Arrange over the cooked rice and drizzle with the sauce.

Yield: 4 servings

A Friend of The Museum of Science and Industry

PIRJANA PILETINA *Croatia*

CHICKEN STEW

1   (3-pound) chicken, with giblets
1   large onion, chopped
1/2   cup mushrooms
3   tablespoons butter
1   tablespoon chopped parsley
    Salt and pepper to taste
1   teaspoon paprika
2   cups chicken broth
2   tablespoons tomato paste

Rinse the chicken and pat dry. Cut into serving pieces. Sauté the onion and mushrooms in the butter in a skillet until the onion is golden brown. Add the parsley, chicken and giblets. Season with salt, pepper and paprika. Pour in the chicken broth. Simmer over low heat until the chicken is tender. Add the tomato paste. Simmer for 10 minutes longer. Serve with rice or dumplings.

Yield: 4 servings

Mary Bonicky, Sacred Heart Croatian School, Kolo and Tambura Group

TAMALES ROJOS *Guatemala*

RED TAMALES

Bananas and beans are typical Guatemalan accompaniments to meats.
Here, the banana leaf is used to "package" the tamale for cooking.

1   (2-pound) chicken

8   tomatoes, skin and
    seeds removed

1   pound miltomates
    (husk tomatoes or
    tomatillos), husks
    removed

2   guaque chiles, cooked

    Ground cloves and
    pepper to taste

1   cinnamon stick,
    broken up

4   hard rolls, soaked in
    milk

$1/4$ teaspoon sesame seeds

$1/4$ teaspoon pumpkin
    seeds

$1/4$ teaspoon achiote seeds
    (annatto)

$1^1/4$ cups shortening

2   pounds (7 cups)
    torti-ya flour or
    masa harina

    Pinch of saffron

2   ounces hard cheese,
    grated

    Banana or plantain
    leaves

Rinse the chicken. Cook in a large stockpot with water to cover until the chicken is tender and cooked through. Remove the meat and set aside; discard the skin and bones. Reserve the cooking broth. Grind the tomatoes, miltomates, chiles, cloves, pepper, cinnamon, bread, sesame seeds, pumpkin seeds and achiote seeds together. Fry the mixture in $1/4$ cup of the shortening in a skillet for 5 to 6 minutes, stirring frequently. Combine with the chicken in a bowl, mixing well. Combine the flour, remaining 1 cup shortening, saffron, cheese and reserved broth in a bowl, stirring to form a soft dough. Shape into flat cakes using 6 tablespoons of the dough. Spoon 2 tablespoons of the tomato filling in the center. Fold up the edges. Wrap the tamales securely in banana leaves and tie up with string. Cook the tamales in a large kettle of boiling water for 3 hours. Remove and drain well before serving; discard the banana leaves before eating.

Yield: 20 to 30 tamales
Consulate General of Guatemala

CHRISTMAS EVE IS THE TIME FOR CELEBRATING IN GUATEMALA, WITH CELEBRANTS STAYING AWAKE TO VIEW THE DAZZLING FIREWORKS THAT FILL THE MIDNIGHT SKY. THEN IT'S TIME TO SIT DOWN TO OPEN PRESENTS AND EAT TAMALES.

MAIN DISHES

ROAST GOOSE WITH GIBLET STUFFING IS TRADITIONAL FARE AT CHRISTMAS IN GERMANY AND SWEDEN. SERVE WITH ROTKRAUT, OR BAVARIAN RED CABBAGE (PAGE 96).

GEBRATENE GANS MIT FÜLLUNG *Germany*

ROAST GOOSE WITH GIBLET STUFFING

1	(9- to 11-pound) goose with giblets
1/3	cup sliced onion
1/4	cup chopped celery
2	chicken bouillon cubes
	Salt and pepper to taste
1/2	cup butter
1/2	cup minced onion
1/2	cup minced celery
2	tablespoons chopped parsley
1	tablespoon poultry seasoning
7	cups cubed bread
1/2	cup milk
2	tablespoons cornstarch

Rinse goose and pat dry. Remove and discard excess fat. Remove the giblets and neck. Place in a small saucepan with water, sliced onion, chopped celery, bouillon cubes, salt and pepper. Bring to a boil; reduce heat. Simmer for 30 to 40 minutes or until the giblets are tender. Remove from the heat and drain, reserving the broth. Chop giblets and neck meat and set aside. Melt the butter in a large saucepan. Add the minced onion, minced celery, parsley, poultry seasoning, salt, pepper and half of the chopped meats, reserving half for the gravy. Cook, covered, over low heat for 12 minutes. Add the bread cubes and milk, tossing well. Rub the goose with salt and pepper inside and outside. Fill the breast cavity loosely with the giblet stuffing. Place the goose breast side down on a rack in a large roasting pan. Cover with foil. Roast at 400 degrees for 1 hour. Remove foil; turn goose breast side up. Reduce oven temperature to 350 degrees and roast, uncovered, for 2 hours longer. Remove from the oven and prick the surface with a fork to release excess fat. Roast, uncovered, for 1 hour longer, until browned and cooked through. If using a meat thermometer, the temperature should be at 170 to 175 degrees. Transfer the goose to a serving platter and let stand for 15 minutes before carving. Skim off and discard the fat from the pan drippings. Add the cornstarch to the reserved broth; stir into the pan drippings. Cook over medium heat until thickened. Stir in the remaining chopped meats and season to taste.

Yield: 6 to 8 servings

Isabella Erbe, Society of the Danube Swabians

MEXICAN PARTRIDGES

6   partridges
1   cup oil
¹/₂ cup vinegar
2   tomatoes, sliced
1   onion, sliced
3   cloves of garlic, chopped
    Thyme, sweet marjoram, salt and pepper to taste
6   hot peppers packed in vinegar, drained

Rinse the partridges and pat dry. Combine oil, vinegar, tomatoes, onion, garlic, thyme, marjoram, salt and pepper in a roasting pan. Add the partridges. Marinate in the refrigerator for 8 to 10 hours, turning occasionally to coat. Cook, covered, over low heat for 25 to 35 minutes or until cooked through. Shake the pan occasionally to prevent sticking, but do not uncover. Let stand for 10 minutes before serving. Garnish with hot peppers.

Yield: 6 servings
Theresa Ochoa, Chicago Mexica Lions Club

MAIN DISHES

IN MEXICO, THE PESEBRE, OR NATIVITY SCENE, IS FOUND IN EVERY HOUSEHOLD. HIGHLIGHTING THE SEASON ARE PARTIES, GAMES, SINGING, AND DANCING, AS WELL AS THE OPPORTUNITY TO TRY TO BREAK THE TREAT-STUFFED PIÑATA.

ROAST TURKEY GUATEMALAN STYLE

1   (8- to 10-pound) turkey
    Salt and pepper to taste
2   tablespoons mustard
¹/₂ cup butter or margarine
¹/₂ cup minced onion
    Bay leaves and basil to taste
    Juice of 15 sweet oranges

Rinse the turkey and pat dry. Discard giblets or set aside for another use. Prick the turkey all over with a fork. Rub with salt and pepper. Refrigerate for 8 to 10 hours. Rub with mustard. Refrigerate for 8 to 10 hours. Rub with butter and onion. Place on a rack in a roasting pan. Add the bay leaves and basil. Pour the orange juice over the turkey. Cover loosely with foil. Roast at 250 degrees until a meat thermometer registers 170 to 175 degrees, or allow 30 minutes per pound. Baste occasionally with the pan drippings. Remove the foil during the last 30 minutes of cooking to allow the turkey to brown.

Yield: 6 to 8 servings
Consulate General of Guatemala

PECHENA RYBA *Ukraine*

BAKED FISH

1	cup grated carrots
1	cup chopped celery
1	cup chopped onion
1	clove of garlic, crushed
1	bay leaf
3	tablespoons oil
1¹/₂	cups canned tomatoes
¹/₂	cup tomato juice
	Salt and pepper to taste
2	pounds lemon sole or flounder fillets
	Lemon juice to taste

Sauté the carrots, celery, onion, garlic and bay leaf in the oil in a skillet until tender. Add the tomatoes. Simmer, covered, for 5 minutes. Add the tomato juice. Process the mixture in a blender or food processor until puréed. Season with salt and pepper. Brush the fish fillets with oil. Sprinkle with lemon juice, salt and pepper. Place in a greased baking dish. Spoon the puréed vegetables evenly over the fish. Bake at 375 degrees for 20 minutes or until fish flakes easily. Garnish with parsley.

Yield: 2 to 4 servings

Ukrainian National Women's League, Branch 22, in Chicago

LYDEKA DREBUCIUOSE *Lithuania*

PIKE IN ASPIC

1¹/₂	pounds soup greens
	Salt, pepper and bay leaf to taste
1	(3- to 4-pound) whole pike, cleaned
1	tablespoon lemon juice or vinegar
2	to 4 envelopes unflavored gelatin
1	hard-cooked egg, thinly sliced
1	carrot, thinly sliced, cooked
	Parsley

Place the soup greens, salt, pepper and bay leaf in a saucepan. Add enough water to cover. Bring to a boil; reduce heat. Simmer for 5 to 10 minutes. Add the fish to the broth mixture. Simmer over low heat for 15 to 20 minutes or until the fish flakes easily. Remove the fish carefully and place in a deep dish or decorative mold. Strain the broth, reserving enough to cover the fish completely (2 to 4 cups). Season the broth with lemon juice and salt. Add the gelatin, using 2 envelopes for each 1 cup of broth. Stir until the gelatin is dissolved. Pour the broth over the fish. Chill, covered, until the gelatin is set. Serve in the dish or turn out mold onto a platter. Decorate with slices of egg, carrot and parsley.

Yield: 4 to 6 servings

Lydia Ringus, Knights of Lithuanian Dancers

Hawaii

MAHI MAHI IN COCONUT MILK

1 1/2 cups coconut milk

1 small onion, chopped

1 small green bell pepper, chopped

Salt to taste

4 mahi mahi fillets

1 tablespoon butter, softened

1 tablespoon flour

1 tomato, chopped

Cayenne pepper to taste

Combine the coconut milk, onion, green pepper and salt in a saucepan. Bring to a boil; reduce heat to medium-low. Add the fish fillets. Poach the fish for 15 minutes or until fish flakes easily. Remove carefully from the liquid and place on a warm platter. Bring the liquid to a boil; reduce the heat to low. Mix the butter and flour in a small bowl. Add to the coconut milk, whisking to remove lumps. Add the tomato, salt and cayenne pepper. Simmer for 2 to 3 minutes or until slightly thickened. Pour over the fish to serve.

Yield: 4 servings

Lynette "Lineaka" Troha, Stars of the South Pacific

MAIN DISHES

THE MAHI MAHI, ALSO KNOWN AS THE DOLPHINFISH OR DORADO, IS FOUND IN WARMER WATERS AND IS ESPECIALLY PLENTIFUL IN HAWAII. ITS FIRM FLESH AND WONDERFUL FLAVOR ARE ACCENTED IN THIS ISLAND RECIPE. OTHER FISH, SUCH AS MULLET OR OPAKAPAKA MAY BE SUBSTITUTED.

SZCZUPAK PO POLSKU *Poland*

NORTHERN PIKE POLISH STYLE

1 carrot

1 rib of celery

1 (2-pound) whole Northern pike, cleaned

1 onion, cut into wedges

10 peppercorns

1 1/2 teaspoons salt

1/4 cup butter, softened

6 hard-cooked eggs, finely chopped

1/4 cup lemon juice

1 tablespoon chopped fresh dill or parsley

3/4 teaspoon salt

1/4 teaspoon pepper

Cut the carrot and celery into 1-inch pieces. Place the fish in a large saucepan. Add the carrot, celery, onion, peppercorns and 1 1/2 teaspoons salt. Add enough water to cover. Bring to a boil; reduce heat to medium. Cook, covered, for 15 to 20 minutes or until the fish flakes easily. Remove the fish carefully with a slotted spoon to a warm platter. Combine the butter, eggs, lemon juice, dill, 3/4 teaspoon salt and pepper in a small bowl. Mix well. Spoon over the fish. Serve with boiled potatoes. May substitute other white fish for Northern pike.

Yield: 4 to 6 servings

Polish Scouting Organization, Z.H.P.—Inc.

DURING THE HOLIDAYS, IT IS
CUSTOMARY FOR YOUNG
PEOPLE IN POLAND TO GO
FROM HOUSE TO HOUSE
SINGING CAROLS WHERE THEY
ARE WELCOMED BY FRIENDS
AND NEIGHBORS.

RYBA W SOSIE CHRZANOWYM *Poland*

FISH IN HORSERADISH SAUCE

2   carrots, coarsely
    chopped

2   ribs of celery, coarsely
    chopped

1   parsley root

1   onion, quartered

1   bay leaf

5   peppercorns

2   teaspoons salt

1^1/2 quarts water

2   pounds carp, sole or
    pike fillets

    Horseradish Sauce

Place the carrots, celery, parsley root, onion, bay leaf, peppercorns, 2 teaspoons salt and water in a large saucepan. Bring to a boil; reduce heat. Simmer for 20 minutes. Strain the stock into a large saucepan. Add the fish. Simmer for 6 to 10 minutes or until the fish flakes easily. Remove the fish gently and place on a serving platter. Chill, covered with plastic wrap. Strain the stock once more, reserving ^{3}/4 cup for the Horseradish Sauce. Spoon the Horseradish Sauce over the fish. Garnish with shredded lettuce.

Yield: 6 servings
Polish Scouting Organization, Z.H.P.—Inc.

HORSERADISH SAUCE

3   tablespoons butter or
    margarine

3   tablespoons flour

^{3}/4 cup strained fish stock

^{3}/4 cup prepared
    horseradish

^{1}/2 teaspoon sugar

^{1}/4 teaspoon salt

^{2}/3 cup sour cream

3   hard-cooked eggs,
    sieved

Melt the butter in a small saucepan. Add the flour, stirring until blended. Add the reserved stock gradually, stirring constantly. Simmer over low heat until the sauce is thick and smooth, stirring constantly. Remove from the heat. Add the horseradish, sugar, ^{1}/4 teaspoon salt, sour cream and eggs; mix well. Let stand to cool for 15 minutes.

TIEBOU DIEUNE *Senegal*
WHITE FISH STEW

1/2 cup chopped hot red peppers

Chopped green onions to taste

2 cloves of garlic, minced

Parsley, bay leaves, salt and pepper to taste

3 1/2 pounds firm white fish

3 large onions, sliced

Oil for sautéing

4 ounces dried fish

1/2 cup tomato purée

3 quarts water

3 large carrots, sliced

1 small cabbage, quartered

1 1/2 cups chopped, peeled cassava root

1 medium sweet potato, peeled, cut into halves

1 cup chopped pumpkin

1 medium eggplant, unpeeled, cut into halves

1 3/4 cups chopped turnips

1 to 2 whole hot red peppers

7 cups rice

Pound the chopped red peppers, green onions, garlic, parsley, bay leaves, salt and pepper in a mortar and pestle until a smooth paste forms, or process in a food processor. Cut a slit in each fish steak and fill with the paste. Sauté the onions in oil in a large skillet until translucent. Add the dried fish and the fish steaks. Cook until the fish is golden brown but not cooked through. Remove to a warmed platter. Combine the tomato purée and water in a large saucepan. Bring to a boil; reduce the heat to medium-low. Add the carrots, cabbage, cassava, sweet potato, pumpkin, eggplant, turnips, whole red peppers and fish. Simmer, covered, for 20 minutes or until all the vegetables are tender. Remove the fish and vegetables with a slotted spoon as they become done and place in a large bowl with a small amount of the cooking broth. Cook the rice in the remaining broth, adding additional water if needed. Spoon the rice onto a large platter. Arrange the fish and vegetables over the rice. Garnish with lemon slices.

Yield: 12 to 14 servings

A Friend of The Museum of Science and Industry

MAIN DISHES

THE CASSAVA USED IN THIS RECIPE IS ALSO KNOWN AS MANIOC OR YUCA. THIS ROOT PLANT IS A STAPLE OF AFRICAN CUISINE AND IS ALSO GRATED FOR USE AS FLOUR OR TAPIOCA.

Main Dishes

THE POBLANO CHILE IS A LARGE DARK GREEN CHILE THAT IS MILDLY SPICY. THEY ARE USUALLY AVAILABLE FRESH IN SUMMER AND FALL, BUT DRIED CHILES MAY BE SUBSTITUTED IF THEY ARE RECONSTITUTED BY SOAKING IN WARM WATER BEFORE USING.

2	poblano chiles
1	pound tomatoes
1	tablespoon minced onion
3	tablespoons oil
	Salt to taste
18	corn tortillas
18	thick slices white cheese
1	cup sour cream

TACOS CON QUESO *Mexico*
CHEESE TACOS

Broil the poblano chiles on a baking sheet in a hot oven until the skin begins to blacken. Remove and place in a paper bag for several minutes to cool. Peel off the skins and remove the seeds. Mash with a little warm water to form a paste. Broil the tomatoes in the same way, removing the skin and seeds. Mash with the chiles and set aside. Sauté the onion in 1 tablespoon of the oil in a skillet until the onion is golden brown. Add the chile-tomato mixture and season with salt. Simmer until the mixture thickens, stirring frequently; remove from the heat. Fry the tortillas in the remaining oil in a skillet until lightly browned and softened. Place the cheese in the middle of each tortilla and roll up to enclose. Place on a serving platter. Pour the chile sauce evenly over the tacos and spoon a dollop of sour cream on each taco. Serve immediately.

Yield: 8 servings

Theresa Ochoa, Chicago Mexica Lions Club

India

SWEET PULLAO

MAIN DISHES

1   onion, thinly sliced

4   to 6 tablespoons ghee
     or oil

4   cardamom pods

6   whole cloves

3   cinnamon sticks

¹/₃ cup golden raisins

¹/₃ cup cashew nuts

2   cups basmati rice,
     rinsed

3¹/₂ cups hot water

6   tablespoons sugar

     Salt to taste

Sauté the onion in ghee or oil in a large deep skillet until golden brown. Remove the onion and set aside. Sauté the cardamoms, cloves and cinnamon for 2 to 3 minutes. Remove and set aside. Sauté the raisins and cashews until the cashews are golden brown. Remove and set aside. Add the rice. Stir-fry until lightly browned, adding additional oil if needed. Add the hot water, cardamoms, cloves, cinnamon, sugar and salt. Cook, tightly covered, over low heat for 20 minutes. Adjust the seasoning in the rice and add a few of the raisins and cashews; stir once. Simmer, covered, over very low heat until all liquid is absorbed, being careful not to burn the rice. Spoon into a serving dish. Top with the sautéed onion and remaining raisins and cashews. Serve with mango or mint chutney.

Yield: 6 to 8 servings

Gertrude Lobo, India Catholic Association of America

"PULAO" OR "PULLAO" IS THE INDIAN VERSION OF A PILAF. SWEET PULLAO OR PLUM PULLAO IS TRADITIONALLY SERVED FOR A BIG FEAST LIKE CHRISTMAS OR EASTER, BUT IS ALSO FOUND AT DINNER PARTIES. BASMATI RICE AND GHEE ARE AVAILABLE AT MOST INDIAN GROCERIES.

Main Dishes

Karelia or Karjala is a region between Finland and Russia. Karelian immigrants to Finland brought this recipe with them. Fishermen and lumbermen often take pasties for lunch. They may be filled with the rice pudding filling at right or with an equal amount of mashed potatoes.

———

Riitta West remembers her mother preparing the boat-shaped pasties every Saturday. Often, during the war, when she had a batch in the oven, the air raid sirens would go off. But because she had heard them so often and because she had already gone through the trouble of getting the oven hot, she continued baking through the bombing!

KARJALANPIIRAKAT *Finland*
KARELIAN RICE PASTIES

¾   cup water
1½ teaspoons salt
1¼ cups rye flour
¾   cup white flour
Rice Pudding Filling
3   tablespoons melted
     butter
Egg Butter

Combine the water, salt and flours in a large bowl. Mix well until a smooth dough forms. Shape the dough into a log about 2 inches in diameter. Cut into 20 equal portions. Shape the portions into flat cakes and roll out to a thin circle. Set aside, but do not stack on top of each other or they will stick together. Place 1½ tablespoons of the Rice Pudding Filling on half of each circle. Fold up the other side and pinch the edges to seal. Place on a nonstick baking sheet. Brush with the melted butter. Bake at 475 degrees for 5 to 7 minutes or until golden brown. Serve the pasties with Egg Butter.

Yield: 20 servings
Riitta M. West

RICE PUDDING FILLING

¾   cup rice
½   teaspoon salt
1½ cups water
¾   cup hot milk
¼   cup butter
1   egg, beaten

Bring the rice and salted water to a boil in a saucepan; stir. Reduce heat to low and cook, tightly covered, until the water is absorbed. Add the milk. Simmer until the milk is absorbed. Add the butter and the egg gradually, stirring well.

EGG BUTTER

4   hard-cooked eggs
½   cup butter, softened
¼   teaspoon salt
¼   teaspoon pepper

Mash the eggs with the butter in a bowl. Season with salt and pepper. Chill slightly in the refrigerator.

VARENYKY *Ukraine*
POTATO-FILLED DUMPLINGS

5   cups flour

1   teaspoon salt

2   tablespoons butter, softened

1   cup evaporated milk

$1/2$ cup water

Potato Filling (at right)

Combine the flour and salt in a large bowl. Add the butter and milk and mix well. Add warm water if needed. Knead the dough lightly on a floured surface. Divide into 4 equal portions. Roll out to $1/8$-inch thickness. Cut into 3-inch circles with a cutter or glass. Place on a floured surface. Cover with a towel to keep from drying out. Place 1 tablespoon of the Potato Filling on one side of the dough circle. Fold over to form a half moon shape, pinching edge to seal. Drop a few at a time into a large kettle of boiling water. Cook until the dumplings rise to the surface. Cook for 3 to 4 minutes longer. Remove with a slotted spoon; place in a colander. Rinse briefly with cold water; drain. Toss with melted butter in a bowl and serve.

Yield: 6 to 8 servings
Ukrainian National Women's League, Branch 22, in Chicago

VERTEENEES *Lithuania*
MEAT DUMPLINGS

3   eggs

1   teaspoon salt

2   tablespoons water

2   cups flour

  Meat Filling (at right)

  Salt to taste

Beat eggs with salt and water in a bowl. Add flour gradually, mixing well. Divide into 3 portions. Roll out on floured surface into 6x14-inch strips of $1/8$-inch thickness. Place Meat Filling on dumpling strips, leaving 1 inch between the patties. Cover with second dumpling strip. Cut with a large round biscuit cutter. Seal edges by pressing with a fork. Drop dumplings into a 3-quart kettle of boiling salted water. Boil for 45 minutes, stirring occasionally. Remove dumplings with a slotted spoon and drain well. Serve with sour cream.

Yield: 6 servings
Lucille VeSota

MAIN DISHES

To prepare the Potato Filling for Varenyky, boil 8 to 9 medium cubed, peeled potatoes in water in a saucepan until tender; drain. Beat well until smooth. Sauté 1 chopped large onion in $1/4$ cup butter or oil in a small skillet until tender. Stir into the potatoes. Season with salt and pepper to taste.

To prepare the Meat Filling for Verteenees, combine $1 1/2$ pounds ground beef, 2 eggs, $1 1/2$ teaspoons salt, $1/4$ teaspoon pepper and 2 tablespoons minced onion in a bowl, mixing well. Shape the mixture into patties using $1/3$ cup at a time.

VUSHKA *Ukraine*

DUMPLINGS WITH MUSHROOM FILLING

2 cups flour

1 teaspoon salt

1 egg yolk

1/2 cup milk or evaporated
  milk

1 teaspoon melted butter
  or oil

  Mushroom Filling

Mix the flour and salt in a large bowl. Add the egg yolk, milk and butter and mix well. Let stand for 5 minutes. Knead for 5 minutes on a floured surface; shape into a ball. Let stand, covered, for 15 minutes. Divide into 3 portions. Roll out each portion on a floured surface to 1/8-inch-thick rectangle. Dust both sides with flour. Cut into 1/2-inch squares and set aside on a floured surface. Place 1 teaspoon of the Mushroom Filling in the center of each dumpling. Fold diagonally to form a triangle; pinch edges to seal. Repeat the process. Bring 2 quarts of water to a boil. Drop in 10 to 12 dumplings at a time. Cook for 1 minute after they float to the top. Remove with a slotted spoon and place on a greased plate to cool. Place 3 to 4 dumplings in a soup bowl and add hot borscht.

Yield: 20 to 30 dumplings

*Ukrainian National Women's League,
Branch 22, in Chicago*

MUSHROOM FILLING

4 ounces dried
  mushrooms

2 pounds fresh
  mushrooms

4 medium onions, finely
  chopped

1 cup butter

1 tablespoon salt

2 teaspoons pepper

1/2 cup bread crumbs

  Juice of 1 lemon

Simmer dried mushrooms in a saucepan with enough water to cover for 1 1/2 hours or until mushrooms are tender, adding water as needed. Remove the mushrooms and set aside to cool; reserve the cooking liquid. Trim the stems and chop the fresh mushrooms. Sauté the onions in butter in a heavy skillet until tender. Add the fresh mushrooms. Cook over medium heat, stirring frequently. Chop the dried mushrooms and add to the mixture. Simmer until liquid has evaporated. Season with salt and pepper. Add the bread crumbs and lemon juice. Remove from the heat. Let stand to cool, stirring frequently to allow steam to escape.

CHAPTER Four

VEGETABLES & SIDE DISHES

A SEASON
of
CELEBRATING

Hanukkah

———⟡———

Hanukkah...what a joyous holiday! Celebrated with songs,
psalms, and feasting by Jewish people throughout the world,
the Festival of Lights, begins in late December on the 25th day
of the Jewish month of Kislev. During the eight days of Hanukkah,
candles are lit on an eight-branched candlestick called a Menorah
to commemorate the legendary miracle of light that occurred
in 165 B.C.E. During Hanukkah, families participate in games,
listen to music, and visit with friends. Gifts are exchanged—
often one for every day of the celebration—something the children
look forward to with great anticipation. Special foods are
enjoyed during this holiday, particularly ones cooked in oil,
such as jelly doughnuts and potato latkes.

PICKLED CABBAGE

KOREAN FOODS ARE
OFTEN LIBERALLY
SPRINKLED WITH CHILI
POWDER, MAKING THEM VERY
SPICY AND PIQUANT.

3   medium Korean cabbages (nappa)

$1/2$ cup salt

2   quarts warm water

$1/4$ cup sweet rice flour or wheat flour

3   cups cold water

2   medium white radishes, thinly sliced

$1/3$ cup red pepper powder

1   tablespoon sugar

2   cloves of garlic, crushed

2   teaspoons crushed gingerroot

5   to 6 green onions, sliced

$2^1/2$ teaspoons salt

2   tablespoons salted baby shrimp

Remove the large outer leaves of the cabbage, leave whole and set aside. Cut the remaining cabbage lengthwise into halves or quarters, but do not separate the leaves. Sprinkle salt between the leaves and place all of the cabbage in a large bowl. Dissolve $1/2$ cup salt in 2 quarts warm water. Pour over the cabbage. Let stand for 2 to 3 hours or until the cabbage softens, turning 2 to 3 times and making sure the cabbage remains submerged. Dissolve the rice flour in 1 cup of the cold water. Bring the remaining 2 cups water to a boil in a saucepan. Add the rice flour mixture. Bring to a boil. Cook until thickened, stirring constantly. Remove from the heat and let stand until cool. Toss the radishes with the red pepper and sugar in a bowl. Add the garlic, gingerroot, green onions, $2^1/2$ teaspoons salt and baby shrimp; mix well. Stir in cooled rice mixture. Rinse the cabbage 3 to 4 times in cold water. Drain, squeezing out excess water. Spoon the radish stuffing mixture between the leaves, beginning with the reserved outside leaves. Wrap with the large outer leaves. Place in a Kim Chi jar (1-gallon jar). Let stand in a cool place for 3 to 4 days. Chill before serving.

Yield: 12 servings

Alycia Wright and Alice Jung

VEGETABLES & SIDE DISHES

ĆWIKLA *Poland*

PICKLED BEETS

3 cups sliced cooked beets

1 tablespoon grated fresh horseradish, or 4 teaspoons prepared horseradish

8 whole cloves, or $^1/_3$ teaspoon caraway seeds

2 cups vinegar

1 tablespoon brown sugar

2 teaspoons salt

Layer the beets in a glass dish, sprinkling each layer with the horseradish and cloves. Combine the vinegar, brown sugar and salt in a saucepan. Bring to a boil. Cook for 2 minutes. Pour over the beets. Chill, covered, for 24 hours before serving.

Yield: 3 cups
Polish Scouting Organization, Z.H.P.—Inc.

Canada

MAPLE SYRUP GLAZED CARROTS

1 pound small carrots
  Salt to taste

2 tablespoons butter

2 tablespoons maple syrup

Cut the carrots into $^1/_8$-inch diagonal slices. Cook in boiling salted water in a saucepan for 6 to 10 minutes; drain well. Melt the butter in a large skillet. Add the carrots; drizzle with the syrup. Cook over low heat for 5 minutes, stirring frequently.

Yield: 4 to 6 servings
The Canadian Women's Club of Chicago

Hungary

BREADED CAULIFLOWER

1   head cauliflower

1   cup margarine

1   cup dry bread crumbs

Separate the cauliflower into flowerets. Place in a saucepan with water to cover. Bring to a boil; reduce heat. Simmer until tender; drain well. Melt the margarine in a large skillet. Add the bread crumbs. Brown lightly. Add the cauliflowerets. Sauté briefly. Serve warm.

Yield: 4 to 6 servings

Margaret Kun, Calvin Reformed Church of Lynwood, Illinois

Canada

FIDDLEHEADS

2   pounds fiddleheads

     Salt to taste

1   cup water

2   tablespoons butter

1   teaspoon vinegar or lemon juice

1/2   teaspoon salt

     Dash of pepper

1   cup 10% cream

2   egg yolks, beaten

1/3   cup shredded Canadian processed cheese

Remove the sheath and scales of the fiddleheads. If the stem is crisp, leave attached. Rinse several times in lukewarm water. Soak in salted cold water to cover for 30 minutes; drain well. Bring 1 cup water to a boil in a saucepan. Add the fiddleheads. Cook for 10 to 15 minutes or until the stalks are tender-crisp; drain. Add the butter, vinegar, salt and pepper, tossing to coat. Combine the cream, egg yolks and cheese in the top of a double boiler. Cook over simmering water until the cheese melts and the sauce is thickened, stirring constantly. Pour over the fiddleheads and serve immediately.

Yield: 4 servings

The Canadian Women's Club of Chicago

VEGETABLES & SIDE DISHES

FIDDLEHEADS ARE THE DELICATE, EDIBLE FRONDS OF THE OSTRICH FERN AND ARE PLENTIFUL IN THE ST. JOHN RIVER VALLEY OF NEW BRUNSWICK. THEY ARE NOW AVAILABLE FROZEN AND HAVE BECOME A CANADIAN GOURMET SPECIALTY. PIONEER WIVES CONSIDERED THEM A GOOD SPRINGTIME TONIC AND PREPARED THEM FOR THEIR FAMILIES, BOILED WITH SALT PORK OR BACON. THE FLAVOR OF THE FIDDLEHEAD IS A CROSS BETWEEN ASPARAGUS AND BROCCOLI. THEY MAY BE SERVED HOT WITH A CHEESE SAUCE, AS IN THE RECIPE AT LEFT, OR COOKED, THEN MARINATED IN A FRENCH DRESSING FOR USE IN SALADS OR AS AN APPETIZER.

VEGETABLES & SIDE DISHES

1 quart water

1/8 teaspoon salt

1 pound beef or chicken
 pieces

1 clove of garlic

1 whole onion

1 cardamom pod

1 whole clove

1 large onion, chopped

1 tablespoon oil

2 (16-ounce) packages
 frozen okra, thawed

1 (8-ounce) can tomato
 sauce

1 tablespoon lemon or
 lime juice

Salt and pepper to taste

Garlic powder, allspice
 and nutmeg to taste

Egypt

OKRA

Bring water and 1/8 teaspoon salt to a boil
in a 2-quart saucepan. Add the beef, garlic,
whole onion, cardamom and clove. Boil until
the beef is cooked through. Remove the beef
with a slotted spoon; set aside to cool. Strain
the broth and reserve, discarding the onion,
garlic and clove. Sauté the chopped onion in
oil in a large deep skillet until the onion is
translucent. Shred the beef and add to the
skillet. Add the okra, tomato sauce and lemon
juice. Sprinkle with salt to taste, pepper, garlic
powder, allspice and nutmeg and stir gently.
Simmer over low heat for 5 minutes. Add 2 to
3 cups of the reserved broth. Simmer, covered,
for 30 to 45 minutes or until the okra is tender,
stirring occasionally and adding additional
broth if necessary. May pour into a baking dish
and bake at 350 degrees for 30 to 45 minutes.

Yield: 6 servings

Mary N. Khair, St. Mark's Coptic Church

Denmark

SUGAR-BROWNED ONIONS

1 pound small pearl
 onions, peeled

2 tablespoons sugar

2 tablespoons butter

Simmer the onions in water to cover in a
saucepan until tender. Drain and rinse in cold
water. Heat the sugar in a nonstick skillet until
the sugar begins to melt and caramelize. Add
the butter. Cook until the butter begins to
bubble in a light brown foam. Add the onions.
Shake the skillet gently to coat the onions in
the caramelized mixture. Cook until golden
brown. Serve immediately.

Yield: 4 servings

*Carol Bach, Danish Sisterhood Society,
Olga Lodge 11*

Belize
OVEN-BAKED PLANTAINS

3   ripe plantains
    Nonstick cooking
      spray

Peel the plantains. Cut into halves crosswise and then slice the halves into 3 portions each. Spray a baking sheet with nonstick cooking spray. Arrange the plantains on the baking sheet and spray them with cooking spray. Bake at 350 degrees for 5 minutes; turn over the plantains. Bake for 10 minutes longer or until tender and a dark rich golden color.

Yield: 6 servings
Enell Thurston, Belizean Cultural Association

VEGETABLES & SIDE DISHES

THE PLANTAIN IS A MEMBER OF THE BANANA FAMILY AND, WHILE IT RESEMBLES THE BANANA, ITS MILD FLAVOR IS SIMILAR TO A SQUASH. IT IS USED EXTENSIVELY IN LATIN AMERICAN AND CARIBBEAN COOKING.

———

SERPENYŐS BURGONYA *Hungary*
PAPRIKA POTATOES

1   large onion, sliced
1/4 medium green bell
      pepper, sliced
3   tablespoons shortening
4   to 5 potatoes, peeled,
      sliced
1 1/2 teaspoons paprika
    Salt and pepper to taste
1/2 to 3/4 cup water

Sauté the onion and green pepper in the shortening in a large deep skillet until the onion is translucent. Add the potatoes. Sprinkle with paprika, salt and pepper. Add the water. Simmer, covered, over medium heat for 25 minutes or until the potatoes are tender. May fry 1 pound of pork sausage links until brown and cooked through and place on the potatoes for a quick main dish meal.

Yield: 4 to 6 servings
Helen Gall, Calvin Reformed Church of Lynwood, Illinois

THE PEPPER PLANT WAS INTRODUCED TO EUROPE DURING THE 16TH CENTURY, PROBABLY FROM TURKEY OR SPAIN. ALTHOUGH PAPRIKA IS KNOWN AS THE HUNGARIAN NATIONAL SPICE, IT WAS NOT USED IN HUNGARIAN RECIPES BEFORE THE 19TH CENTURY. THERE ARE AT LEAST FIVE DIFFERENT VARIETIES OF PAPRIKA, RANGING FROM HOT (FROM GREEN PEPPERS OR ROSE-RED PEPPERS) TO SWEET AND MILD. MOST PAPRIKA USED IN COOKING IS MILDER THAN CAYENNE OR CURRY. IN ADDITION TO ADDING FLAVOR TO DISHES, PAPRIKA IS ALSO RICH IN VITAMINS A AND C AND IS BENEFICIAL FOR THE DIGESTIVE SYSTEM.

VEGETABLES & SIDE DISHES

THE FOLLOWING RECIPES FROM ISRAEL, THE CZECH REPUBLIC, BELARUS, ECUADOR AND MEXICO OFFER SLIGHTLY DIFFERENT VARIATIONS ON THE POTATO PANCAKE, OR "LATKE," A STAPLE ITEM ON THE MENU OF MANY COUNTRIES.

———

FOODS COOKED IN OIL, SUCH AS DOUGHNUTS AND POTATO PANCAKES, ARE PART OF THE HANUKKAH FESTIVAL OF LIGHTS. THE RECIPE FOR NOUVELLE LATKES COMBINES THE TRADITIONAL INGREDIENTS WITH NEW ONES FOR A DIFFERENT "GOURMET" FLAVOR. ENJOY AND SAVOR THEM AS A REMINDER OF THE RELIGIOUS FREEDOM SHARED BY PEOPLE OF ALL FAITHS AND BELIEFS IN THE UNITED STATES.

Israel
NOUVELLE HANUKKAH LATKES

6	medium high-starch potatoes, peeled
1	medium onion
6	eggs, beaten
1/2	cup matzo meal
1/4	teaspoon freshly ground pepper
1/8	teaspoon freshly ground nutmeg
1	(10-ounce) package frozen chopped spinach, thawed and drained
1/2	cup vegetable or olive oil for sautéing

Grate the potatoes and onion and place in a colander. Let stand to drain, pressing to remove excess water; pat with paper towels. Combine the eggs, matzo meal, pepper and nutmeg in a bowl, beating until smooth. Stir in the spinach, mixing well. Add the drained potato mixture. Heat the oil in a large skillet until a drop of water sizzles in the pan. Pour the potato mixture 1/4 cup at a time into the skillet, leaving 1 inch between the latkes. Sauté for 3 minutes or until the edges are browned; turn and cook the other side for 3 minutes. Remove to paper towels to drain. Keep warm until serving time. Serve with sour cream, plain yogurt or applesauce.

Yield: 8 servings

Rabbi Ira S. Youdovin, Chicago Board of Rabbis

Israel
TRADITIONAL LATKES

6	baking potatoes, peeled
2	eggs, slightly beaten
1/4	cup flour
1/2	teaspoon baking powder
1/2	teaspoon salt
1/2	teaspoon pepper
	Dash of nutmeg
2	cups grated onions
	Vegetable oil for frying

Grate the potatoes into a large bowl. Cover with cold water. Drain well and pat dry with paper towels. Combine with the eggs, flour, baking powder, salt, pepper, nutmeg and onions. Let drain in a strainer for 5 minutes. Heat the oil in a large skillet. Shape the potato mixture into patties. Cook in the prepared skillet over medium heat until browned on 1 side; turn. Cook until browned and cooked through. Drain on paper towels. Serve with applesauce and/or sour cream.

Yield: 6 to 8 servings

Judy Kupfer

BRAMBORÁK *Czech Republic*

POTATO PANCAKES

2½ pounds potatoes, peeled
Salt to taste
Milk
1 to 2 eggs, beaten
1 cup flour
¾ cup shortening

Grate the potatoes. Place in a colander over a large bowl; sprinkle with salt. Let stand to drain, reserving the drained liquid. Measure the reserved liquid and add the same amount of milk. Combine with the potatoes, eggs and flour in a bowl; mix well. Heat the shortening in a large skillet. Drop the potato mixture by spoonfuls into the hot skillet. Fry on each side until golden brown.

Yield: 4 to 6 servings
Club Bedrich Smetana

Belarus

RAISED YEAST POTATO PANCAKES

1½ envelopes dry yeast
1 tablespoon sugar
¼ cup warm water
2 medium potatoes
1 egg, beaten
1 to 2 cups milk
2 tablespoons sour cream
3 tablespoons sugar
1 teaspoon salt
5 to 6 cups flour
Vegetable oil for frying

Dissolve the yeast with 1 tablespoon sugar in the warm water. Boil the potatoes in water to cover in a saucepan until tender. Drain, reserving the cooking liquid. Peel the cooled potatoes. Place in a bowl with a small amount of the reserved liquid. Mash until smooth and thick. Add the yeast mixture, egg, 1 cup of the milk, sour cream, 3 tablespoons sugar and salt, mixing well. Add the flour 2 cups at a time, stirring well after each addition until the dough is firm and elastic. Add more milk if necessary. Shape into round pancakes. Fry in hot oil until browned on both sides. Serve with sour cream.

Yield: 4 to 6 servings
Sofia Latuszkin, Belarusian American National Council of Chicago

VEGETABLES & SIDE DISHES

DRANICKI ARE TRADITIONAL BELARUSIAN TREATS AND ARE SERVED IN EVERY VILLAGE, ESPECIALLY FOR HOLIDAYS. KNOWN AS "DRANICKI" IN SOME REGIONS, IN OTHERS THEY ARE CALLED "BULBIANYJA BLINY."

DRANICKI IS MADE BY GRATING 10 LARGE PEELED POTATOES AND 2 LARGE ONIONS IN A FOOD PROCESSOR. COMBINE WITH 2 TABLESPOONS FLOUR AND SALT AND PEPPER TO TASTE IN A LARGE BOWL. DROP THE POTATO MIXTURE INTO HOT OIL BY SPOONFULS. FRY ON EACH SIDE UNTIL GOLDEN BROWN.

YIELD: 8 TO 10 SERVINGS

LOLIYA KANTAROVICH, BIELARUSIAN COORDINATING COMMITTEE OF CHICAGO

VEGETABLES & SIDE DISHES

LLAPINGACHOS ARE ORIGINALLY FROM THE ANDEAN CITIES, BUT ARE WELL KNOWN ALL OVER ECUADOR AND ARE POPULAR FOR ANY OCCASION. AS A SIDE DISH, SERVE WITH ROAST PORK OR BEEF AND A FRESH SALAD, OR SERVE AS APPETIZERS.

———

DUMPLINGS (PAGE 93) ARE ANOTHER FAVORITE ON MANY TABLES AROUND THE WORLD. IN GERMANY, DUMPLINGS MAY BE FILLED WITH FRUIT, VEGETABLES, MEAT, FISH OR CHEESE AND OFTEN TAKE THE PLACE OF BREAD. THEY ARE SERVED AS SOUP ACCOMPANIMENTS, MAIN DISHES OR EVEN DESSERTS. KNOWN AS PIEROGI IN POLAND, AND PIROZHKI OR PELMENY IN BELARUS, DUMPLINGS ARE FILLED WITH CHOPPED MEAT OR VEGETABLES OR MAY BE FILLED WITH FRUIT AND SERVED AS DESSERT. THE RECIPES HERE ARE VARIATIONS ON THE EVER-POPULAR POTATO DUMPLING.

LLAPINGACHOS *Ecuador*
POTATO PANCAKES

4 to 5 pounds white potatoes, peeled

Salt to taste

16 ounces Mexican white cheese, shredded

Corn oil for frying

Boil the potatoes with water to cover in a saucepan until tender; drain well. Mash with salt in a bowl until smooth. Let stand to cool for 5 to 10 minutes. Shape the mixture into 2-inch balls. Insert 1 spoonful of the cheese in the center of each. Flatten into pancakes. Fry in a small amount of hot oil until golden brown on each side.

Yield: 6 to 8 servings

Rosa Mata and Ximena Bastidas,
Chicago Ecuadorean Lions Club

TORTAS DE PAPA CON GUACAMOLE *Mexico*
POTATO PATTIES WITH GUACAMOLE

The avocado is a favorite accompaniment in Mexico. Ripe avocados are often spread over bread for a snack.

3 large potatoes

250 grams (8.75 ounces) corn dough

100 grams (3.5 ounces) shredded cheese

Oil for frying

3 ripe avocados, peeled, seeded

1 tablespoon grated onion

1 tomato, chopped

Cooked chicken strips

Steam the potatoes in a steamer until tender; cool and peel. Mash in a bowl with the corn dough and cheese. Shape the mixture into patties. Heat the oil in a skillet. Fry the patties until golden brown on each side. Drain on paper towels. Mash the avocados with the onion and tomato in a small bowl to make the guacamole. Top the potato patties with the guacamole and strips of cooked chicken.

Yield: 4 to 6 servings

Theresa Ochoa, Chicago Mexica Lions Club

Lithuania

BASIC POTATO DUMPLINGS

Peel and grate 7 potatoes. Strain through a clean cloth, catching the liquid in a bowl. Allow the liquid to settle and pour off carefully, reserving only the starchy sediment. Mix the potatoes, the reserved starch, 1 chopped onion, 1 beaten egg, salt and pepper to taste and $^1/_4$ cup flour in a bowl, mixing thoroughly. Shape into small balls. Drop a few at a time into boiling, salted water. Boil for 30 minutes. Remove with a slotted spoon and drain well. Serve with melted butter or chopped, fried bacon and minced onion.

Yield: 6 servings
Barb VeSota

KARTOFFELKNÖDEL *Germany*

POTATO DUMPLINGS

Boil 2 pounds of red potatoes in salted water for 20 to 25 minutes, drain and rinse with cold water. Chill for 8 to 10 hours. Peel and grate 4 pounds of raw potatoes into a bowl of cold water. Strain through cheesecloth into a bowl, reserving the white starchy sediment. Peel and grate the cooked red potatoes. Mix with the raw potatoes. Stir in the reserved starch, $^1/_4$ cup farina, 1 tablespoon salt and $^3/_4$ cup hot milk. Fry 1 hard roll, cubed, in 1 tablespoon butter until brown. Fold into mixture. Shape $^1/_4$ cup of the mixture at a time into balls. Drop into a saucepan of boiling, salted water. Cook for 10 to 15 minutes or until dumplings rise to the top. Remove with a slotted spoon and serve hot.

Yield: 8 servings
Isabella Erbe, Society of the Danube Swabians

PIEROGI *Poland*

FILLED DUMPLINGS

Make a well in the center of 2 cups flour on a floured surface. Drop in 2 beaten eggs and $^1/_2$ teaspoon salt. Add $^1/_3$ cup water. Work the flour into the center until all liquid is absorbed. Knead until the dough is firm. Let rest, covered, for 10 minutes. Divide into halves. Roll each half very thinly. Cut into 3-inch rounds. Place a teaspoon of filling to 1 side of the round; fold, pressing edges to seal with a small amount of water. Drop into boiling salted water. Cook for 3 to 5 minutes or until the pierogi float to surface. Remove with slotted spoon and drain. Serve with melted butter or sautéed onion.

Yield: 15 to 24 pierogi
Polish Scouting Organization, Z.H.P.—Inc.

VEGETABLES & SIDE DISHES

PIEROGI ARE WELL KNOWN EVERYWHERE. THEY ARE NOT, STRICTLY SPEAKING, POTATO DUMPLINGS, ALTHOUGH THEY MAY BE FILLED WITH POTATOES. FOR A POTATO FILLING, MASH 2 TO 3 COOKED POTATOES WITH 1 TO 2 TABLESPOONS FINELY CHOPPED ONION AND $^1/_2$ CUP GRATED CHEESE.

———————

FOR CABBAGE FILLING, MIX 2 CUPS CHOPPED, COOKED CABBAGE WITH 1 CUP PREPARED SAUERKRAUT, CHOPPED SAUTÉED ONION AND $^1/_4$ CUP COOKED CHOPPED MUSHROOMS.

———————

FOR DESSERT PIEROGI, FILL WITH COOKED PRUNES AND SERVE WITH SOUR CREAM OR YOGURT.

Vegetables & Side Dishes

Throughout Polynesia, tuber root plants such as the sweet potato, kumara and taro are main staples in the diet. They are served boiled, mashed, pounded (as in poi) or baked in an earthen oven (an imu). This Sweet Potato Casserole is from my Kumu Hula (Master Hawaiian Dance Instructor) at a family luau in Laie, Oahu, Hawaii.

Hawaii

Sweet Potato Casserole

1	tablespoon butter
4	large sweet potatoes, peeled, parboiled, sliced
4	bananas, peeled, sliced
4	apples, peeled, cored, sliced into rings
1 1/2	cups coconut milk
1/2	cup brandy or rum
2	tablespoons freshly chopped mint

Grease a shallow baking dish with the butter. Layer the sweet potatoes, bananas and apples in the baking dish. Mix the coconut milk, brandy and mint in a small bowl. Pour over the layers. Bake, covered, at 350 degrees for 20 minutes. Bake, uncovered, for 10 minutes longer to brown.

Yield: 6 to 8 servings

Lynette "Lineaka" Troha, Stars of the South Pacific

African American

Sweet Potato Pancakes

3	medium sweet potatoes
1	small onion
1	egg, beaten
2	tablespoons flour
1/2	teaspoon salt
	Dash of pepper
1/4	teaspoon baking powder

Peel the sweet potatoes and finely grate into a bowl. Grate the onion and mix with the sweet potatoes. Stir in the egg. Combine the flour, salt, pepper and baking powder. Add to the sweet potato mixture. Drop by heaping tablespoonfuls into a greased, preheated nonstick skillet. Fry for 4 minutes on each side or until cooked through. Serve with applesauce, apple butter or sour cream and chives.

Yield: 4 to 6 servings

Angela Cole

African American
MIXED GREENS

2 bunches mustard
    greens or kale

2 bunches turnip greens

1 teaspoon salt, or
    to taste

   Pepper to taste

Rinse the mustard and turnip greens well; remove the stems. Bring water to a boil in a 3-quart saucepan. Add the greens. Cook, covered, over medium heat for 25 minutes or until tender. Drain, reserving a small amount of the cooking liquid (called "pot liquor"). Season greens with salt and pepper. Serve with the reserved liquid. May add 2 tablespoons cooked ham, bacon or turkey to the greens before serving.

Yield: 8 servings
Angela Cole

VEGETABLES & SIDE DISHES

GREEN LEAFY VEGETABLES ARE A GOOD SOURCE OF VITAMINS A AND C. THE MIXTURE OF THE PUNGENT MUSTARD-FLAVORED GREENS WITH THE SLIGHTLY SWEETER TURNIP GREENS MAKES FOR A HEALTHY, FLAVORFUL DISH.

Si Gum Chi Na Mul *Korea*
SESAME SPINACH

1 pound fresh spinach

1 quart water

1 teaspoon soy sauce

1 tablespoon sesame oil

2 teaspoons sesame seeds

1/2 clove of garlic, finely
    crushed

1 green onion, chopped

1/8 teaspoon pepper

Rinse the spinach well. Bring the water to a boil in a 2-quart saucepan. Add the spinach. Cook for 1 minute; remove from the heat. Rinse with cold water and drain well, squeezing out excess water. Place in a serving bowl. Mix the soy sauce, sesame oil, sesame seeds, garlic, green onion and pepper in a small bowl. Pour over the spinach, tossing to coat. Garnish with a sprinkling of chopped nuts.

Yield: 8 servings
Alycia Wright and Alice Jung

THE COMBINATION OF VEGETABLES WITH FRUIT IS ONE OF THE DISTINGUISHING CHARACTERISTICS OF GERMAN COOKING. THIS RED CABBAGE DISH IS USED AS A VEGETABLE ACCOMPANIMENT FOR GERMAN CHRISTMAS GOOSE.

BAYERISCHES ROTKRAUT *Germany*

BAVARIAN RED CABBAGE

4	slices bacon
1	medium onion, chopped
4	cups shredded red cabbage
1	tart apple, peeled, chopped
1	tablespoon sugar
1/2	teaspoon salt
1/8	teaspoon pepper
1/4	teaspoon caraway seeds
3	tablespoons cider vinegar

Cook the bacon in a deep skillet until crisp. Remove all but 2 tablespoons of the pan drippings. Sauté the onion in the drippings until tender. Add the cabbage, apple, sugar, salt, pepper and caraway seeds; mix well. Cook, covered, over low heat for 10 minutes. Stir in the vinegar. Cook for 15 minutes longer.

Yield: 8 servings

Marianne B. Schroeder, Society of the Danube Swabians

KAPUSTA I GROCH *Poland*

SAUERKRAUT WITH PEAS

This dish used to be served at Polish weddings.

1	cup whole dried yellow peas
3	dried mushrooms
2	quarts sauerkraut
1	onion, chopped
3	tablespoons butter
	Salt and pepper to taste

Soak the peas in water to cover in a saucepan for 10 to 12 hours. Cook in the soaking liquid over medium heat for 1 hour. Soak the mushrooms in water to cover in a small bowl for 4 hours. Chop coarsely and set aside. Rinse and drain the sauerkraut, squeezing to remove excess liquid. Chop coarsely. Place in a large saucepan with water to cover. Bring to a boil. Add the mushrooms and onion. Simmer for 1 hour. Drain the peas; add to the sauerkraut mixture. Cook for 30 minutes longer. Stir in the butter, salt and pepper before serving.

Yield: 8 to 10 servings

Joan Pitchford, Lansing Business Women's Association

SHAKSHOUKA *Israel*
EGGS IN TOMATO SAUCE

1   large onion, finely chopped

     Oil for sautéing

6   medium tomatoes

4   eggs

     Salt and pepper to taste

Sauté the onion in a small amount of oil in a large skillet until slightly browned. Grate the tomatoes coarsely. Add to the onion. Cook, covered, over low heat for 25 minutes. Break the eggs over the mixture, stirring gently to break the yolks. Cook, covered, for 3 to 4 minutes or until the eggs are set. Season with salt and pepper to serve. May also add minced garlic or chopped red pimentos when sautéing.

Yield: 4 servings

Embassy of Israel and Consulate General of Israel to the Midwest

VEGETABLES & SIDE DISHES

LESHAKSHEK MEANS "TO SHAKE" IN HEBREW, AND THIS DISH IS A SEPHARDI FAVORITE. NO MIDDLE EASTERN MENU IS COMPLETE WITHOUT IT, AND HUNGARIANS ALSO PREPARE IT, ADDING LOTS OF PAPRIKA. IN FACT, ALL NORTH AFRICAN COOKS HAVE THEIR OWN INDIVIDUAL VERSION OF THIS EGG AND TOMATO DISH. THE ONLY REQUIREMENT IS THAT THE VEGETABLES MUST BE FRESH, NOT CANNED.

POMIDORAI IDARYTI GRYBAIS *Lithuania*
TOMATOES STUFFED WITH MUSHROOMS

10   medium tomatoes

      Salt and pepper to taste

1   large onion, finely chopped

1/2   cup oil

1 1/2   pounds fresh mushrooms, chopped, or 8 ounces dried mushrooms

2   tablespoons dry bread crumbs

Rinse and dry the tomatoes. Cut off the tops and reserve; scoop out and discard seeds and pulp. Sprinkle the tomato shells with salt and pepper; set aside. Sauté the onion in a small amount of the oil in a skillet until golden brown. Add the remaining oil. Add the chopped mushrooms, bread crumbs, salt and pepper. Sauté until the mushrooms are tender. Spoon the mixture into the tomato shells. Cover with the reserved tomato tops, securing with wooden picks. Arrange in a baking dish, leaving space between the tomatoes. Bake at 300 degrees for 15 to 20 minutes, checking frequently. Do not overbake or tomato skins will split. Remove from the oven and baste with pan juices. Let stand until cooled. Serve cold.

Yield: 10 servings

Lydia Ringus, Knights of Lithuanian Dancers

Vegetables & Side Dishes

Greeks love vegetables and serve a wide variety with their daily meals. This dish is special because it offers a combination of vegetables.

———

Rice has been a staple food in Korea for more than 1000 years, and is generally served three times a day, except in summer, when it is often replaced by buckwheat noodles served in a cold soup. There are many different varieties of rice grown in Korea. Unhusked rice is especially rich in protein, minerals and vitamins.

TOURLOU *Greece*

Baked Mixed Vegetables

$^1/_4$	cup melted butter
$1^1/_2$	cups hot water
$^1/_4$	cup olive oil
	Pinch each of garlic salt and dried dillweed
	Salt and pepper to taste
1	medium eggplant
4	ounces okra
6	to 8 ounces green beans
3	medium tomatoes, peeled, sliced
2	small zucchini, peeled, sliced
2	large green bell peppers, chopped
2	onions, chopped
1	cup tomato sauce
$^1/_4$	cup water

Combine the butter, $1^1/_2$ cups water, olive oil, garlic salt, dillweed and salt and pepper to taste into an 8x12-inch baking dish. Slice the eggplant and cut into 1-inch strips lengthwise. Trim the tops from the okra. Remove the ends from the green beans. Layer the eggplant, tomatoes, zucchini, okra, green peppers, green beans and onions in the baking dish. Mix the tomato sauce with $^1/_4$ cup water. Pour over the layers. Bake at 350 degrees for 40 minutes or until the vegetables are tender.

Yield: 10 servings
Anna Livaditis, Peiraikon Hellenic School

BOB *Korea*

Boiled Rice

2	cups short grain rice
$2^1/_2$	cups water

Rinse the rice 3 to 4 times in cold water. Place in a heavy saucepan. Add the water. Bring to a boil over medium-high heat; stir once. Cook, covered, for 1 minute; reduce the heat to low. Simmer for 10 to 15 minutes; turn off the heat. Let stand, covered, for 15 to 20 minutes to steam.

Yield: 6 servings
Alycia Wright and Alice Jung

Belize

RICE AND BEANS

1	cup dried red kidney beans
4	ounces salted meat, chopped
1	clove of garlic, chopped
1	cup thick coconut cream
1	onion, sliced
	Salt and pepper to taste
2	cups rice

Soak the beans in water for 8 to 10 hours. Drain and place in a large saucepan with enough water to cover. Bring to a boil; reduce the heat to medium. Simmer for 30 to 40 minutes. Add the salted meat and garlic. Cook until the beans are tender but still whole. Add the coconut cream, onion, salt and pepper. Rinse the rice. Add to the bean mixture. Simmer over low heat until all liquid is absorbed, stirring occasionally and adding water if needed. Serve hot with a meat dish.

Yield: 4 servings
Helen Gabourel, Belizean Cultural Association

VEGETABLES & SIDE DISHES

CHINESE VEGETABLES ARE CUT INTO DIAGONAL STRIPS, CUBED OR SHREDDED TO COOK QUICKLY AT HIGH HEAT YET RETAIN THEIR CRISPNESS. WHEN THE VEGETABLES HAVE BEEN STIR-FRIED FOR A MINUTE OR SO, A SMALL AMOUNT OF LIQUID IS ADDED TO THE PAN. IN THIS WAY THE VEGETABLES COOK RAPIDLY BUT DO NOT BECOME SOFT.

ARHAT DISH _China_

MIXED STIR-FRY VEGETABLES

4	dried mushrooms
1/2	carrot, peeled
1	lily bulb
40	grams (1.4 ounces) pea pods
	Facai (seaweed)
40	grams (1.4 ounces) wheat flour gluten
1	tablespoon sesame oil
1	bamboo shoot
6	pieces miniature corn
2	tablespoons vegetarian oyster sauce
1	teaspoon sugar
	Pepper to taste
1	teaspoon cornstarch
1	cup vegetarian soup stock

Soak the mushrooms in water until softened; drain. Slice the mushrooms, discarding the stems. Boil the carrot in water in a saucepan until tender. Drain and slice. Rinse the lily bulb and the pea pods. Soak the facai and gluten in water until soft. Stir-fry the mushrooms in oil in a skillet. Add the bamboo shoot, carrot, lily bulb, corn and pea pods 1 ingredient at a time. Stir-fry until tender-crisp. Stir in the facai mixture, oyster sauce, sugar, pepper to taste and cornstarch mixed with the soup stock. Simmer until all the liquid has evaporated, stirring occasionally. Serve hot.

Yield: 2 to 4 servings
Liang Chiung-pai

Native American
NATIVE WILD RICE

This is a traditional Chippewa dish.

1   cup chopped scallions

1   cup sliced mushrooms

1   pound wild rice

2   chicken bouillon cubes

     Salt and pepper to taste

1/2   cup slivered almonds,
       or 3 slices crisp-fried
       bacon, crumbled

Sauté the scallions and mushrooms in a small skillet for 10 minutes. Rinse the rice thoroughly. Combine with the scallions and mushrooms in a baking dish. Add the bouillon cubes and enough water to cover. Bake at 375 degrees for 45 minutes. Season with salt and pepper and top with almonds or bacon. Bake for 15 minutes longer.

Yield: 6 to 8 servings

Vonda Gluck (Chippewa),
Native American Tree Committee

China
YANG CHOW FRIED RICE

1/2   cup peeled, cooked
       shrimp

1   teaspoon cornstarch

1   tablespoon white wine

3   tablespoons oil

1   tablespoon minced
       scallion

2   tablespoons lard or
       shortening

5   eggs, beaten

6   cups cooked rice

1   teaspoon salt

1/2   cup chicken stock

1/2   cup Charshu (page 56)

1   cup chopped cooked
       chicken

1/2   cup frozen peas,
       thawed

Toss the shrimp with the cornstarch and wine in a small bowl. Fry in 1 tablespoon of the oil in a small skillet for 1 to 2 minutes; remove and set aside. Sauté the scallion in the remaining oil until slightly browned; remove and set aside. Melt the lard in a large skillet. Add the beaten eggs. Cook until firm and dry. Add the rice, scallion and salt. Simmer for 5 minutes, stirring constantly and adding chicken stock as needed. Add the shrimp, Charshu and chicken. Simmer until heated through. Add the peas. Simmer for 2 to 3 minutes longer, stirring frequently.

Yield: 6 servings

Ginger Cheung, Chinese American Civic Council

Egypt
RICE WITH NUTS

2   cups white rice

Dash of cinnamon and powdered cloves

6   ounces chopped walnuts

6   ounces chopped pecans

6   ounces pine nuts

6   ounces raisins

Cook the rice using package directions, seasoning with the cinnamon and cloves. Combine the walnuts, pecans, pine nuts and raisins in a small bowl. Stir into the rice mixture. Spoon into a serving dish. May add the nut mixture to the rice halfway through the cooking time. Spoon into a baking dish and bake at 300 degrees until the liquid is absorbed. The nuts may also be arranged over the rice on a serving platter for decoration.

Yield: 6 to 8 servings

Mary N. Khair, St. Mark's Coptic Church

O-MISOKA SOBA *Japan*
BUCKWHEAT NOODLES

2   cups dashi (soup powder)

3   to 4 tablespoons soy sauce

1/2   teaspoon sugar

1/4   teaspoon MSG

2   green onions, finely chopped

1   daikon (white radish), grated

1   (16-ounce) package soba (buckwheat noodles)

2   sheets nori (dried seaweed), toasted, crumbled

Sliced kamaboko (fish cake), tempura, or blanched spinach

Combine the dashi, soy sauce, sugar and MSG in a saucepan. Bring to a boil. Add the green onions and daikon. Remove from the heat and let stand to cool slightly. Pour the sauce into a small bowl to serve with the noodles. Boil the noodles in water in a saucepan until tender. Drain and rinse with cold water. Place in a serving bowl. Sprinkle with the nori and garnish with kamaboko, tempura or blanched spinach. Serve with the daikon sauce for dipping.

Yield: 4 to 6 servings

Tampopo-Kai

VEGETABLES & SIDE DISHES

SPAETZLE (MEANING "LITTLE SPARROW" IN GERMAN) ARE TINY EGG NOODLES, OR DUMPLINGS. THEY ARE SERVED AS A SIDE DISH, OFTEN WITH MELTED BUTTER OR GRAVY.

———

THIS STUFFING IS A FAVORITE IN MARGARET KUN'S FAMILY, PASSED DOWN TO HER FROM HER MOTHER, WHO LEARNED IT FROM HER MOTHER, AND ON AND ON . . . . HELEN GALL SUGGESTS PUSHING THE STUFFING UNDER THE SKIN OF A ROASTING CHICKEN. IT'S BEAUTIFUL, BROWN AND DELICIOUS.

2	eggs
$^1/_2$	cup milk
$1^1/_2$	cups flour
$^1/_2$	teaspoon salt
2	to 3 tablespoons butter

Germany
SPAETZLE

Beat the eggs with the milk in a medium bowl. Add the flour and $^1/_2$ teaspoon salt, stirring with a wooden spoon until a smooth dough forms. Fill a large stockpot $^2/_3$ full of water; add 1 teaspoon salt per quart of water used. Bring to a boil; reduce heat to low or medium, for a gentle, rolling boil. Drop $^1/_2$ teaspoonfuls of the dough into boiling water. Dip the spoon into the boiling water each time so the spaetzle will fall off easily. Cook until the spaetzle rise to the top. Remove with a slotted spoon to a colander. Rinse with cold water and drain. Melt the butter in a saucepan. Add the spaetzle, turning to coat. Serve with Chicken Paprikash (page 67).

Yield: 4 to 6 servings

Maria Kreiling, Society of the Danube Swabians

TOLTELÉK *Hungary*
STUFFING

1	loaf dry Vienna bread
6	eggs, beaten
1	medium onion, minced
$^1/_4$	cup freshly chopped parsley
$^1/_2$	cup finely chopped celery
	Salt, pepper and paprika to taste
$^1/_2$	cup margarine, melted
3	to 4 chicken livers, chopped
1	(10-ounce) can chicken broth

Soak the bread in water. Squeeze out and chop coarsely. Combine with the eggs, onion, parsley, celery, salt, pepper and paprika in a large bowl; mix well. Stir in the melted margarine and chicken livers. Add a small amount of broth to moisten. Spoon into a buttered baking dish. Pour remaining broth over the top. Bake at 350 degrees for 30 to 40 minutes or until browned.

Yield: 6 servings

Margaret Kun, Calvin Reformed Church of Lynwood, Illinois

CHAPTER Five

BREADS & GRAINS

A SEASON
of
CELEBRATING

Kwanzaa

—◈—

Unity...Self-determination...Collective work and Responsibility...
Cooperative Economics...Purpose...Creativity...Faith...
these are the seven principles on which Kwanzaa, an African American
cultural holiday, is based. Created by Dr. Maulana Karenga in 1966,
Kwanzaa was conceived from African harvest celebrations called
"the first fruits" and is meant to reaffirm and strengthen the bonds
between African Americans. This seven-day celebration begins on
December 26th and lasts until January 1st. It is a time for families
and friends to spend time together focusing on one's role in life.
Each evening during Kwanzaa, a candle is lit on a seven-tiered
candelabra called a Kinara. When the candle is lit, one of the seven
principles is discussed. In many homes, relevant items are displayed
to represent the principles of Kwanzaa. Zawadi, or gifts,
are exchanged on the last night and special foods are served
throughout the holiday.

BLINCYKI NADZIAVANYJA HRYBAMI *Belarus*
MUSHROOM CRÊPES

1   cup flour
$^1/_2$ teaspoon salt
2   eggs
1   egg yolk
1   cup milk
2   tablespoons water
2   tablespoons melted
     butter
3   tablespoons oil
     Mushroom Filling
$^1/_2$ cup shredded Swiss
     cheese

Sift the flour and salt together. Beat the eggs, egg yolk, milk, water and melted butter in a mixer bowl. Add the flour mixture and mix well. Heat 1 teaspoon of the oil in a skillet over medium heat. Swirl 3 tablespoons of the batter over the bottom of the skillet. Brown on both sides. Repeat the process with the remaining batter. Spoon $1^1/_2$ tablespoons of the Mushroom Filling in the center of each crêpe. Roll up and place seam side down in a baking dish. Bake at 350 degrees for 20 minutes. Reheat the remaining Mushroom Filling and spoon over the crêpes. Sprinkle with the cheese. Broil until light brown.

Yield: 8 to 10 servings

Elizabeth Kulas, Bielarusian Coordinating Committee of Chicago

MUSHROOM FILLING

$1^1/_2$ pounds mushrooms,
     sliced
1   onion, sliced
4   tablespoons butter
2   tablespoons flour
2   cups whipping cream
$^1/_4$ teaspoon salt
     Nutmeg, cayenne and
     white pepper to taste

Sauté the mushrooms and onion in 2 tablespoons of the butter in a skillet until the mushrooms are light brown. Melt the remaining 2 tablespoons of butter in a saucepan. Add the flour, stirring until blended. Add the cream slowly, stirring constantly. Stir in the salt, nutmeg, cayenne and white pepper. Cook over low heat until thickened, stirring constantly. Adjust the seasonings. Add $^1/_2$ to $^2/_3$ of the cream sauce to the mushroom mixture, stirring just until moistened.

BREADS & GRAINS

BLINIS, BLINCYKI, BLINTZES, CRÊPES, CRESPELLES, PFANNKUCHEN, PALACSINTA, PALAČINK, PANNUKAKKU, HOTTOKEEKI, TIGANI'TA, CLĂTITĂ, PANDEKAGE, PANNEKOEK, LÍVANEC, NALEŚNIK, TORTILLAS, HOE CAKES, FLAPJACKS... WHATEVER THE LANGUAGE, WE'RE TALKING ABOUT PANCAKES. THEY CAN BE FILLED WITH CHEESE, FISH, MEAT OR VEGETABLES AND SERVED WITH A SAUCE FOR A MAIN DISH MEAL, OR SPRINKLED WITH SUGAR OR CHOCOLATE, DRIZZLED WITH JELLY OR SYRUP, OR TOPPED WITH SOUR CREAM OR WHIPPED CREAM FOR DESSERT. SURELY THE MOST VERSATILE AND WORLDLY OF ANY DISH. THE FOLLOWING RECIPES ALL BEGIN WITH A BASIC PANCAKE, BUT USE SLIGHTLY DIFFERENT INGREDIENTS WHICH RESULT IN DIFFERENT TEXTURES, FROM PAPER-THIN CRÊPES TO THICK AND HEARTY GRIDDLE CAKES. AS FOR THE FILLINGS, THERE IS NO LIMIT TO WHAT CAN BE USED.

Breads & Grains

Welsh Cakes are a type of unfilled cake-like pancake that are tasty just as they are and made by mixing 2 cups flour, $^3/_4$ cup sugar, $2^1/_2$ teaspoons baking powder, $^1/_2$ teaspoon salt, $^1/_2$ cup softened butter, 2 beaten eggs, 1 teaspoon cinnamon or nutmeg, $^3/_4$ cup currants or raisins and $^1/_4$ cup milk in a bowl. Chill for 1 hour. Pat $^1/_8$ inch thick on a lightly floured surface. Cut into 2- to 3-inch rounds. Fry in a lightly greased skillet until browned on both sides. Sprinkle with additional sugar and serve warm.

Yield: 16 servings

Ellenor Williams
Cambrian Benevolent
Society of Chicago

Israel
CHEESE BLINTZES

This recipe uses a very thin batter to produce a pancake resembling the traditional French crêpes. Mix 2 cups dry cottage cheese, 3 ounces softened cream cheese, 1 egg and 2 to 3 tablespoons of sugar in a bowl. Stir in cinnamon and raisins to taste; set aside. Combine 1 cup flour, $^1/_4$ teaspoon salt, 1 cup water (or milk) and 2 beaten eggs in a bowl, stirring until smooth. Drop 2 to 3 tablespoons of the batter into a hot lightly greased crêpe pan, tilting the pan to spread the batter over the bottom. Brown on one side only. Remove to a towel. Spread with $1^1/_2$ tablespoons cheese filling. Bake in a baking dish at 300 degrees for 10 minutes.

Yield: 25 servings
Embassy of Israel and Consulate General of Israel to the Midwest

Croatia
PALAČINKE

Palačinke also calls for a thin batter. Beat 4 eggs in a bowl. Add 1 cup milk, $^3/_4$ cup flour, 2 tablespoons sugar and $^1/_4$ teaspoon salt; mix well. Let stand for 1 hour. Spread $^1/_4$ cup batter in a lightly greased 7-inch crêpe pan. Brown lightly on each side. Fill with a mixture of 4 cups cottage cheese, $^1/_2$ cup sour cream and $^1/_4$ cup sugar, using 2 tablespoons per Palačinke. Top with sour cream. Bake in a buttered baking dish at 350 degrees for 5 minutes.

Yield: 8 to 10 servings
Ann Simunovic-Goetz, Sacred Heart Croatian School, Kolo and Tambura Group

Lithuania
VAREKECIA

Varekecia also use a cheese filling made with 16 ounces dry cottage cheese, 2 eggs, 1 tablespoon sour cream and a dash of salt and sugar. The pancake batter is made by combining 1 cup flour, $^1/_2$ teaspoon salt and 3 beaten eggs. Stir in 1 cup of milk slowly, then add $^1/_4$ cup melted butter. Drop 2 tablespoons of the batter onto a hot greased skillet, tilting the pan. Brown on one side only. Fill with 1 tablespoon of the cheese filling; roll up. Place seam side down in a buttered baking dish. Bake at 350 degrees for 5 minutes. Serve with sour cream.

Yield: 10 to 12 servings
Bernice Kasarski

Scotland
SCOTCH PANCAKES

Scotch Pancakes are made with buttermilk and are rich and thick, yet their texture is light and airy due to the baking powder and cream of tartar. These are not filled, but may be served with butter, sugar, jam or syrup, or simply plain. Combine 2 cups flour, $^1/_2$ teaspoon baking soda, 1 teaspoon cream of tartar, 1 teaspoon baking powder, $^1/_2$ teaspoon salt, $^1/_4$ cup sugar, 3 tablespoons softened butter, 3 beaten eggs and 1 cup (about) buttermilk and mix until a stiff batter forms. Drop by tablespoonfuls onto a hot greased griddle. Bake on both sides until lightly brown.

Yield: 10 to 12 servings
Pat LeNoble, Thistle & Heather Highland Dancers

Belarus
APPLE PANCAKES

Belarusian Apple Pancakes (called *Aladacki z jablykami*) are a delicious treat. Beat 2 eggs with $^3/_4$ cup milk and 1 tablespoon oil. Stir in 1 tablespoon sugar, $^1/_2$ teaspoon salt and 1 teaspoon vanilla extract. Add $1^1/_2$ cups flour gradually, stirring until smooth. Fold in 2 peeled and grated Granny Smith apples. Drop by spoonfuls onto a hot greased griddle. Fry until browned on each side. Serve with sour cream and sugar or sprinkle with confectioners' sugar.

Yield: 8 to 10 servings
Anna Bruszkiewicz and Lucy Jalamov, Bielarusian Coordinating Committee of Chicago

Sweden
SWEDISH PANCAKES

In Sweden, the pancakes are called "*Plättar*" and are cooked in a "*plättpanna*," producing an even, round shape. A heavy cast-iron skillet, a crêpe pan or a griddle may also be used. *Plättar* are usually served for breakfast or a light supper. Beat 3 eggs with 1 cup cream in a mixer bowl. Sift in 1 cup flour, beating until smooth. Add 2 cups milk gradually. Stir in $^1/_4$ cup melted butter, $^1/_4$ teaspoon salt, and, if desired, 1 tablespoon sugar. Drop 2 tablespoons of the batter onto the heated greased pan, tilting the pan to spread the batter evenly. Brown on each side. Repeat the process with the remaining batter. Serve with sugar, lingonberry jam and light cream.

Yield: 4 large servings
Aina Momquist, Linnea South Suburban Swedish Women's Club

BREADS & GRAINS

FOR A VARIATION ON THE THIN PANCAKES, TRY SWEDISH OVEN PANCAKES. BEAT 2 EGGS WITH 1 CUP MILK. ADD $^1/_2$ TEASPOON SALT, 2 TEASPOONS SUGAR AND $1^1/_2$ CUPS SIFTED FLOUR, STIRRING UNTIL SMOOTH. MIX IN $1^1/_2$ CUPS MILK. LET STAND FOR 10 MINUTES; STIR. POUR INTO A BUTTERED 8x12-INCH BAKING DISH. BAKE AT 400 DEGREES FOR 30 MINUTES OR UNTIL GOLDEN BROWN AND PUFFED. CUT INTO SQUARES AND SERVE IMMEDIATELY WITH FRUIT, JAM OR SYRUP.

YIELD: 10 TO 12 SERVINGS

VIRGINIA HAST, LINNEA SOUTH SUBURBAN SWEDISH WOMEN'S CLUB

BREADS & GRAINS

KUTIA *Ukraine*

WHEAT AND POPPY SEED PUDDING

*Served at the beginning of the Christmas Eve festivities
in the Ukraine and in Belarus.*

2	cups wheat berries (whole kernels)
3/4	cup poppy seeds
1/2	cup chopped nuts (optional)
	Honey to taste

Sift through the wheat berries, discarding any foreign matter; rinse well. Spread in a baking pan. Bake at 250 degrees for 45 minutes, stirring occasionally. Let stand to cool slightly. Place in a paper bag and beat with a rolling pin to loosen the bran from the berry. Rinse thoroughly and place in a saucepan with enough water to cover. Simmer for 2 hours or until tender. Rinse the poppy seeds and place in a bowl. Cover with boiling water. Let stand for 15 minutes; drain well. Process in a food processor until finely ground. Stir into the cooked wheat, adding the nuts and honey.

Yield: 4 to 6 servings

Ukrainian National Women's League, Branch 22, in Chicago

AVIZINIS KISIELIUS *Lithuania*

OATMEAL PUDDING

*This is one of the twelve traditional dishes served during the
Lithuanian Christmas Eve dinner.*

3	cups oat flour
6	cups warm water
1	slice black bread
	Salt to taste
	Dried fruit, sliced (optional)

Combine the oat flour with warm water in a large container. Add the black bread. Let stand, covered, in a warm place for 12 to 20 hours or until soured. Mix well and strain into a large saucepan. Add the salt and fruit. Simmer over low heat until the mixture thickens, stirring occasionally. Pour into a lightly greased mold. Chill until set. Serve with Poppy Seed Milk (page 12) or with sweetened milk.

Yield: 18 servings

Lydia Ringus, Knights of Lithuanian Dancers

BAZLAMACA *Croatia*
CORN BREAD

16 ounces creamed
cottage cheese

$^1/_2$ cup sugar

2 eggs

$^1/_2$ teaspoon salt

$^1/_4$ cup margarine,
softened

$^1/_2$ cup cornmeal

$^1/_2$ cup flour

$^1/_4$ teaspoon baking soda

1 cup sour cream

1 cup buttermilk

Mix the cottage cheese with the sugar, eggs and salt in a bowl. Add the margarine, cornmeal, flour, baking soda, sour cream and buttermilk, stirring until moistened. Spoon the batter into a greased 9x9-inch baking pan. Bake at 425 degrees for 30 to 45 minutes or until browned.

Yield: 9 servings

Emma Tezak, Sacred Heart Croatian School, Kolo and Tambura Group

BREADS & GRAINS

ON DECEMBER 13 (ST. LUCY'S DAY) IN CROATIA, FAMILIES PLANT SEEDS OF GRAIN IN SMALL BOWLS OF WATER SO THAT THEY CAN PLACE THE SPROUTED PLANTS UNDER THE CHRISTMAS TREE ON CHRISTMAS EVE. THE PLANTS ARE THEN PLACED ON DINING TABLES NEXT TO CANDLES AND LOAVES OF BREAD.

Native American
INDIAN FRY BREAD

There are many recipes for the most famous of all American Indian foods. This is a Southwestern recipe that is often served at holidays or family celebrations.

2 cups flour

3 tablespoons (heaping)
baking powder

$^1/_4$ teaspoon salt

$^1/_4$ cup sugar (optional)

Warm water

Shortening for
deep-frying

Combine the flour, baking powder, salt and sugar in a bowl. Add the warm water gradually, stirring until a stiff dough forms. Knead for several minutes and shape into a ball. Let rise for 20 to 30 minutes. Roll $^1/_4$ to $^1/_2$ inch thick on a lightly floured surface. Cut into 2-inch squares. Heat the shortening in a skillet. Deep-fry the squares in the hot shortening until browned on both sides, turning once. Serve warm with honey.

Yield: 12 servings

Sharon Skolnick (Apache), Native American Tree Committee

BREADS & GRAINS

THESE SCONES FROM
SCOTLAND ARE TRADITIONALLY
SERVED AT AFTERNOON
TEA OR "THREESIES."

Ireland

NORA'S IRISH SCONES

4	cups flour
1	teaspoon baking soda
2	teaspoons baking powder
$1/4$	teaspoon salt
$3/4$	cup sugar
$1/2$	cup butter
$1^1/2$	cups raisins or raisins and currants
1	egg
$1^1/2$	cups buttermilk

Combine the flour, baking soda, baking powder, salt and sugar in a large bowl. Cut in the butter until crumbly. Add the raisins. Beat the egg with the buttermilk in a small bowl. Add to the flour mixture and stir with a wooden spoon. Knead lightly on a floured surface. Roll $3/4$ inch thick. Cut into 3-inch rounds with a biscuit cutter. Arrange on a greased baking sheet. Bake at 400 degrees for 20 to 25 minutes or until lightly browned.

Yield: 20 to 24 scones

Nora Murphy, Irish American Heritage Center

Scotland

SCOTCH SCONES

3	cups flour
1	teaspoon baking soda
$1/2$	teaspoon baking powder
$1/2$	cup plus 2 tablespoons sugar
$3/4$	teaspoon salt
$1/4$	cup butter
$1/4$	cup lard
1	egg, lightly beaten
$2/3$	cup milk

Combine the flour, baking soda, baking powder, sugar and salt in a bowl. Cut in the butter and lard. Beat the egg with the milk in a bowl. Add to the flour mixture, cutting in quickly with a knife. Shape the dough into a ball; divide into 2 equal portions. Roll each portion $1/2$ inch thick on a lightly floured surface. Cut into 4 equal portions. Heat a skillet over medium-high heat. Dust with flour. Cook the scones for 5 minutes or until browned on each side, turning once. Repeat with the remaining dough, wiping skillet and reflouring between batches.

Yield: 8 scones

Pat LeNoble, Thistle & Heather Highland Dancers

A SEASON OF CELEBRATING

Ireland

WHOLE WHEAT BREAD

2 cups all-purpose flour

2 cups whole wheat flour

1 teaspoon baking soda

1 teaspoon baking powder

1/4 teaspoon salt

1/2 cup packed brown sugar

1 egg

1/4 cup melted butter

1 1/2 cups buttermilk

Combine the flours, baking soda, baking powder, salt and brown sugar in a large bowl. Beat the egg, butter and buttermilk together in a small bowl. Stir into the flour mixture, mixing with a wooden spoon until the dough forms a ball. Place the ball of dough in a greased 9-inch baking pan. Bake at 375 degrees for 45 to 50 minutes or until loaf tests done.

Yield: 1 round loaf

Nora Murphy, Irish American Heritage Center

BREADS & GRAINS

ON CHRISTMAS EVE, CANDLES ARE LIGHTED AND PLACED IN EVERY WINDOW OF THE HOUSE, AND DOORS ARE LEFT AJAR. THESE ARE SYMBOLS OF WELCOME AND HOSPITALITY, ASSURING THE IRISH PEOPLE THAT THE BABY JESUS WILL NOT BE HOMELESS. THE CANDLES MUST SHINE ALL NIGHT AND CAN ONLY BE EXTINGUISHED BY THOSE HAVING THE NAME MARY.

Ireland

IRISH BROWN BREAD

1 (15-ounce) package seedless raisins

1/4 cup butter or margarine

3 eggs, lightly beaten

3 1/2 cups flour

1 cup sugar

2 teaspoons baking soda

1/2 teaspoon salt

1/2 teaspoon allspice

1/2 teaspoon nutmeg

1 1/2 teaspoons cinnamon

Simmer the raisins in water to cover in a saucepan for 15 minutes. Drain, reserving 1 cup of the cooking liquid. Combine the reserved liquid, raisins and butter in a large bowl. Let stand until cool. Stir in the eggs. Sift the flour, sugar, baking soda, salt, allspice, nutmeg and cinnamon together. Add to the raisin mixture, stirring until a soft dough forms. Spoon into a 10-inch tube pan. Bake at 350 degrees for 1 hour or until loaf tests done. Turn out on a rack to cool completely.

Yield: 1 loaf

Kay Shevlin, Irish American Heritage Center

BREADS & GRAINS

GREAVES OR "GRIEBEN,"
ARE KNOWN IN AMERICA AS
"CRACKLINGS." THEY ARE
SMALL PIECES OF PORK SKIN
THAT HAVE BEEN SALTED AND
CRISP-FRIED. THEY ARE ALSO
POPULAR IN SWEDEN. THESE
BISCUITS ARE CRUNCHY AND
FLAKY AND MAY BE BAKED
WITH A TOPPING OF SALT
AND CARAWAY SEEDS AND
CUT INTO ROUNDS, SQUARES
OR TRIANGLES FOR USE
AS APPETIZERS.

Belize
CREOLE BREAD

1	tablespoon dry yeast
1	teaspoon sugar
1/4	cup warm water
8	cups flour
2	teaspoons salt
1/2	cup lard
	Cream of 1 coconut

Dissolve the yeast and sugar in the warm water. Combine the flour and salt in a bowl. Cut in the lard. Stir in the yeast mixture. Add the coconut cream gradually, stirring until a soft dough forms. Knead on a floured surface for 10 to 15 minutes. Place in a greased bowl, turning to coat the surface. Let rise, covered, until doubled in bulk. Punch down and knead for 5 to 10 minutes. Shape into desired form. Place on a greased baking sheet. Let rise, covered, until doubled in bulk. Bake at 350 degrees for 40 to 50 minutes or until the loaf is browned and sounds hollow when tapped.

Yield: 1 loaf

Olga Bradley, Belizean Cultural Association

Germany
GREAVE BISCUITS

1	envelope dry yeast
1	teaspoon sugar
1	cup warm milk
3	cups flour
1	teaspoon salt
1	teaspoon baking powder
1	cup ground greaves (cracklings)
1/2	cup margarine
1	egg, beaten
	Salt to taste
	Caraway seeds

Dissolve the yeast and sugar in the warm milk. Combine the flour, 1 teaspoon salt, baking powder and greaves in a large bowl. Cut in the margarine until the mixture is crumbly. Add the yeast and milk mixture, stirring until a smooth dough forms. Roll 1/2 to 3/4 inch thick on a lightly floured surface. Cut with a 2-inch biscuit cutter. Place on a baking sheet. Make a lattice indentation on the top of each biscuit with the back of a knife. Brush with the egg. Sprinkle with salt and caraway seeds. Bake at 400 degrees for 30 minutes.

Yield: 18 biscuits

Eva Pfaff, Society of the Danube Swabians

A SEASON OF CELEBRATING

BOZICNJAK *Serbia*

DECORATED CHRISTMAS SWEET BREAD

This bread is placed as a centerpiece on the Christmas table, next to the holiday candle, where it remains for the duration of the holidays. It is cut on New Year's Day and shared by family and friends.

BREADS & GRAINS

1	cup warm milk
1	teaspoon sugar
1	envelope dry yeast
1	to 2 tablespoons flour
1	cup milk
1	cup unsalted butter
3	egg yolks
1	teaspoon salt
1	tablespoon sugar
4	cups flour
1	egg, beaten
3	egg whites, lightly beaten

Combine 1 cup warm milk, sugar, yeast and 1 to 2 tablespoons flour in a medium bowl; stir. Let stand to rise. Scald 1 cup milk in a saucepan over medium heat; remove from heat. Add the butter, stirring until melted. Let cool slightly. Beat the egg yolks in a bowl. Add to the milk gradually, beating constantly. Combine with the salt, 1 tablespoon sugar and 4 cups flour in a large bowl. Add the yeast mixture, stirring to mix. Remove ⅛ of the dough for decorations and set aside. Place the remaining dough in a greased bowl, turning to coat. Let stand, covered, until doubled in bulk. Punch the dough down and knead for 5 minutes. Shape into a ball. Place in a greased 9-inch round baking pan with 3-inch sides. Let rise until doubled in bulk. Prepare the decorations with the unrisen dough as directed at right. Brush the top of the bread only with 1 whole beaten egg. Brush the decorations with any remaining egg white. Bake at 350 degrees for 45 to 60 minutes or until golden brown and the loaf sounds hollow.

Yield: 1 loaf

Miryana Trbuhovich, Federation of Circles of Serbian Sisters, Midwestern Metropolitanate of the Serbian Orthodox Church

TO DECORATE CHRISTMAS SWEET BREAD, SEPARATE HALF OF THE UNRISEN DOUGH INTO 3 EQUAL PORTIONS. ROLL INTO THIN ROPES AND BRAID TOGETHER; JOIN THE ENDS. ARRANGE AROUND THE TOP CIRCUMFERENCE OF THE BREAD AND BRUSH WITH EGG WHITE TO ADHERE. PLACE A CROSS IN THE CENTER OF THE CIRCLE. FLATTEN A SMALL PORTION OF THE DOUGH INTO A 2-INCH SQUARE. FOLD UP AS FOR A BLANKET, LEAVING ONE END OPEN. PLACE A SMALL BALL OF DOUGH REPRESENTING THE HEAD OF THE CHRIST CHILD AT THE OPEN END. USE 2 PEPPER-CORNS FOR THE EYES. PLACE THIS IN THE CENTER OF THE CROSS. ROLL A STRIP OF DOUGH TO A 3-INCH LENGTH. TIE A KNOT WITH ONE END SHORTER THAN THE OTHER. FLATTEN THE LONG END AND MAKE SEVERAL SLITS WITH A KNIFE TO REPRESENT A BIRD'S TAIL. PINCH THE OPPOSITE END TO SHAPE A BIRD'S HEAD, USING PEPPERCORNS FOR THE EYES. ARRANGE ON THE BREAD AROUND THE CROSS, BRUSHING WITH EGG WHITE TO ADHERE. MAY ALSO DECORATE WITH BUNCHES OF GRAPES, STALKS OF WHEAT, OR CHURCH SEALS.

At the Christmas meal
this Serbian bread is
blessed by the head of
the household who then
breaks off the first piece,
and offers it to the rest
of the family. The Cesnica
is never cut with a knife.
The person who finds
the coin will be the bearer
of good fortune in the
coming year.

CESNICA *Serbia*

LUCKY COIN CHRISTMAS BREAD

1	envelope dry yeast or 1 cake yeast
$^1/_2$	cup warm water
2	eggs, beaten
1	teaspoon salt
$^1/_2$	cup butter, softened
$1^1/_2$	cups warm milk
5	to $5^1/_2$ cups flour, sifted
1	sterilized silver dollar
	Vegetable oil

Dissolve the yeast in warm water in a large
bowl. Add the eggs, salt, butter and warm milk,
beating well. Add flour gradually. Knead the
dough for 15 to 20 minutes or until smooth
and elastic. Place in a greased bowl, turning to
coat the surface. Let rise, covered, for 1 to $1^1/_2$
hours or until doubled in bulk. Punch down
and knead again for 5 minutes. Insert the silver
dollar into the dough. Shape the dough into a
ball and place in a greased round baking pan.
Let rise, covered, for 45 minutes. Brush the top
with a small amount of oil. Bake at 350 degrees
for 1 hour or until golden brown. Remove to a
wire rack to cool completely.

Yield: 1 loaf

*Gordana Trbuhovich, Federation of Circles of Serbian
Sisters, Midwestern Metropolitanate of the Serbian
Orthodox Church*

KIFLI *Hungary*

FILLED ROLLS

1	envelope dry yeast
1	tablespoon sugar
$^1/_2$	cup warm milk
1	pound (2 cups) butter, softened
4	cups (heaping) flour
1	cup sour cream
5	egg yolks, beaten
	Butter-flavor shortening
	Chopped nuts or apricot butter
1	egg yolk, beaten

Dissolve the yeast and sugar in warm milk. Cut
the butter into the flour in a bowl until crumbly.
Add the yeast mixture, sour cream and 5 egg
yolks. Knead until smooth and elastic. Shape
into 4 balls. Roll out very thinly on a floured
surface. Brush with shortening. Fold into thirds
and roll up. Wrap loosely in plastic wrap. Chill
for 8 to 10 hours. Roll out each portion. Cut
into $2^1/_2$-inch squares or triangles. Spread with
nuts or apricot butter. Fold over to enclose
filling, sealing edges. Place on a baking sheet.
Brush with 1 egg yolk. Bake at 350 degrees for
20 minutes or until browned.

Yield: 24 rolls

*Margaret Kun, Calvin Reformed Church of
Lynwood, Illinois*

KIRMESKUCH *Luxembourg*
SWEET BREAD

For Madeleine Thomé, the Kirmes, a yearly festival to commemorate the consecration of a church, was always looked forward to because it meant getting together with friends and relatives, eating fabulous meals, and above all, tasting this warm, sweet bread spread with butter.

**BREADS
& GRAINS**

$3^1/2$ **to 4 cups flour**

$^1/2$ **cup sugar**

1 **envelope dry yeast**

$^1/2$ **teaspoon salt**

$^1/2$ **cup butter**

$^1/3$ **cup milk**

$^1/4$ **cup water**

3 **eggs, beaten**

$^1/2$ **cup raisins (optional)**

Combine 1 cup of the flour, sugar, yeast and salt in a large mixer bowl. Heat the butter, milk and water in a small saucepan to 120 degrees. Stir into the dry ingredients gradually. Beat at high speed for another 2 minutes. Add the eggs and $^1/2$ cup of the flour. Beat for 2 minutes longer. Add enough of the remaining flour gradually, stirring to form a soft dough. Let rise, covered, in a warm place until doubled in bulk. Punch down and turn onto a floured surface. Divide into 2 equal portions. Knead on floured surface for 1 to 2 minutes. Shape into loaves. Place in 2 buttered and floured 5x9-inch loaf pans. Let rise, covered, for 1 hour or until doubled in bulk. Bake at 350 degrees for 30 minutes or until loaves test done. Cool on a wire rack. Store, wrapped in plastic wrap, in the refrigerator.

Yield: 2 loaves
Madeleine Thomé

KOLACH *Ukraine*

Braided Bread

1 teaspoon sugar

1 envelope dry yeast

1/3 cup lukewarm water

2 eggs

1 egg yolk

1 teaspoon salt

2 tablespoons sugar

2 tablespoons vegetable oil

1/2 cup lukewarm water

4 cups sifted flour

1/3 cup seedless raisins (optional)

1 egg, beaten

Sprinkle 1 teaspoon sugar and the yeast over 1/3 cup lukewarm water. Let stand until foamy. Beat 2 eggs, the egg yolk, salt, 2 tablespoons sugar, oil and 1/2 cup lukewarm water in a large bowl. Stir in the yeast mixture. Add the flour gradually, stirring well. Knead until the dough is smooth and elastic. Place in a greased bowl, turning to grease the surface. Let rise, covered, in a warm spot for 1 to 1 1/2 hours or until doubled in bulk. Punch down and let rise until doubled in bulk. Knead on a floured surface for 5 minutes, adding the raisins if desired. Divide the dough into 6 equal portions. Shape each portion into a 26-inch rope. Braid 2 of the strips together, starting at the center. Repeat with the remaining dough, ending with 3 sets of braids. Braid 2 of the sets together, starting in the center. Join the ends of the strips to form a circle. Place in a greased 9-inch round baking pan, leaving a 1/2-inch space between the braid and the pan and placing a small greased can in the middle to keep the center open. Place the remaining braided portion around the outside edge of the braided circle, joining the ends. Let rise, covered, until doubled in bulk. Brush with 1 egg. Bake at 375 degrees for 10 minutes; reduce the oven temperature to 350 degrees. Bake for 40 minutes longer or until golden brown.

Yield: 1 loaf

Ukrainian National Women's League, Branch 22, in Chicago

SAFFRANSBRÖD *Sweden*

SAFFRON BREAD

1/2	teaspoon saffron
1	cup lukewarm cream or milk
2	envelopes dry yeast
1/3	cup sugar
1/2	teaspoon salt
1	egg, beaten
1/2	cup melted butter or margarine
1/2	cup raisins
4	cups (about) sifted flour
1	egg, beaten

Spread the saffron in a small baking pan. Dry in the oven at very low temperature for 2 to 3 minutes. Crush the saffron in a small bowl until powdery. Spoon 1 tablespoon of the warm cream over the saffron and let stand. Dissolve the yeast in the remaining warm cream in a large bowl. Add the sugar, salt, 1 egg, butter, raisins, saffron and 1/2 of the flour. Stir with a wooden spoon until the flour is incorporated. Add the remaining flour gradually, stirring until a smooth dough forms. Knead on a floured surface for 10 minutes. Place in a buttered bowl, turning to grease the surface. Let rise, covered, in a warm place for 1 1/2 hours or until doubled in bulk. Punch down the dough and knead gently for 1 to 2 minutes. Pinch off portions of the dough. Roll out on a floured surface into 7-inch long strips. Pinch 2 strips together in the center, curling the ends. Place a raisin in each curl. May also use 3 strips, or 1 thick strip with the ends rolled into an S-shaped bun. May also shape into braided loaves or a ring. Place the buns on a buttered baking sheet. Let rise, covered, for 45 minutes or until doubled in bulk. Brush with 1 egg. Bake at 400 degrees for 10 to 15 minutes.

Yield: 20 buns

Aina Momquist, Linnea South Suburban Swedish Women's Club

IT IS UNUSUAL THAT THIS EXOTIC SPICE, USED SO MUCH IN THE RICE DISHES OF THE ORIENT, HAS FOUND ITS WAY TO THIS NORTHERN COUNTRY. THE SAFFRON IS KNEADED INTO A SWEET DOUGH WHICH IS SHAPED INTO ARTISTICALLY SHAPED BUNS CALLED "LUSSEKATTER" IN SWEDISH. THE AROMA OF FRESHLY BAKED SAFFRON BREAD SIGNALS THE BEGINNING OF THE SWEDISH CHRISTMAS SEASON, WHICH IS DECEMBER 13, ST. LUCIA'S DAY. THE ELDEST DAUGHTER IN THE FAMILY DRESSES IN A WHITE GOWN WITH A RED SASH AND PLACES AN EVERGREEN CROWN WITH NINE CANDLES ON HER HEAD. SHE WAKES THE FAMILY WITH COFFEE AND SAFFRON BREAD. THE DAY ENDS WITH THE SELECTION OF THE LUCIA QUEEN AND A PARADE.

BREADS & GRAINS

CHRISTMAS BREAD

A well-known and great favorite at Christmas time.

1½ cups raisins

1 cake yeast

½ cup lukewarm milk

4 cups sifted flour

1 cup butter or margarine, softened

½ cup sugar

2 eggs

½ cup milk

Grated peel of ½ lemon

½ teaspoon salt

¼ teaspoon nutmeg

1 cup chopped almonds

Melted butter

¾ cup confectioners' sugar

3 to 4 teaspoons milk

Steam the raisins until plumped; drain and set aside. Dissolve the yeast in ½ cup lukewarm milk in a medium bowl. Stir in 1 cup of the flour. Let rise, covered, in a warm place. Cream 1 cup butter and sugar in a large mixer bowl until light and fluffy. Add the eggs 1 at a time, beating well after each addition. Add ½ cup milk, lemon peel and the yeast mixture, mixing well. Add the remaining 3 cups flour, salt and nutmeg. Knead the mixture until the dough is smooth and elastic. Knead the raisins and almonds into the dough. Place the dough in a greased bowl, turning to coat the surface. Let rise, covered, in a warm place until doubled in bulk. Roll out slightly on a floured surface. Brush with melted butter. Make an indentation in the center of the dough using a rolling pin. Fold in half to form a long loaf. Place on a greased baking sheet. Brush with melted butter. Let rise, covered, until doubled in bulk. Bake at 350 degrees for 40 minutes or until the loaf tests done. Place on a wire rack to cool slightly. Beat the confectioners' sugar with 3 to 4 teaspoons milk in a bowl until a smooth glaze forms. Drizzle over the loaf.

Yield: 1 large or 2 small loaves
Maria Kreiling, Society of the Danube Swabians

Hungary

POPPY SEED ROLLS

2	envelopes dry yeast
3	tablespoons sugar
3/4	cup warm milk
1	cup margarine
5	cups flour
4	egg yolks, lightly beaten
1	cup sour cream
2	cups poppy seeds
4	egg whites
1	cup sugar
1	teaspoon vanilla extract
	Grated lemon peel
1	egg white, beaten
1	to 2 teaspoons water

Dissolve yeast and 3 tablespoons sugar in warm milk in bowl. Cut margarine into flour in bowl until crumbly. Stir in egg yolks, sour cream and yeast mixture. Let stand for 30 minutes. Grind poppy seeds. Beat 4 egg whites, 1 cup sugar and vanilla in a mixer bowl until soft peaks form. Fold in poppy seeds and lemon peel. Fold egg white mixture into flour, until soft dough forms. Divide dough into 4 equal portions. Roll out. Spread poppy seed mixture evenly on each portion; roll up. Place on a baking sheet. Let rise until doubled in bulk. Brush with a mixture of 1 egg white and water. Bake at 350 degrees for 45 to 60 minutes or until rolls are golden brown.

Yield: 4 rolls

Margaret Kun, Calvin Reformed Church of Lynwood, Illinois

Czech Republic

BOHEMIAN NUT ROLLS

3	eggs, beaten
1	cup sour cream
2	cakes yeast
1/2	cup warm milk
6	cups flour
1	teaspoon salt
5	tablespoons sugar
1	cup butter, softened
2	pounds walnuts
1	egg white
1 1/2	cups sugar
1 1/2	tablespoons vanilla extract
1	egg yolk, beaten

Mix eggs and sour cream in a bowl. Chill, covered, for 8 to 10 hours. Dissolve the yeast in the warm milk. Mix the flour, salt and 5 tablespoons sugar in a bowl. Cut in the butter until crumbly. Add the sour cream and yeast mixtures and mix well. Grind the walnuts. Beat the egg white in a large mixer bowl until foamy. Fold in the walnuts, 1 1/2 cups sugar and vanilla. Divide the dough into 4 portions and roll out on a floured surface. Spread the walnut mixture in the center of each portion. Roll up. Place on a greased baking sheet. Let rise, covered, for 2 hours. Brush with egg yolk. Bake at 350 degrees for 35 to 40 minutes.

Yield: 4 rolls

Joseph Straka

BREADS & GRAINS

AT MIDNIGHT IN HUNGARY, TOWNSPEOPLE, DRESSED IN BRIGHT COSTUMES, MEET AT CHURCH TO CELEBRATE MASS. THEY ARE SURROUNDED BY CANDLES, FLOWERS AND EVERGREENS AS WELL AS A BEAUTIFUL CRECHE ON DISPLAY.

Breads & Grains

In Croatia, the sweet, fragrant perfume of Orehnjaca wafts through the house on Christmas morning. Although the bread is traditionally served after the Christmas dinner, it is difficult to resist sampling it straight from the oven early in the morning. This recipe is one that Croatians carry with them wherever they may go and is passed down from generation to generation. Mary Tomacic received the recipe from her mother and will in turn pass it on to her daughters. She hopes that you will enjoy it as much as they do.

Orehnjaca *Croatia*

WALNUT ROLL

1¹/₂	cakes yeast
8	tablespoons sugar
1	cup warm milk
5	to 6 cups flour
1	egg, beaten
3	egg yolks
¹/₂	cup melted butter
¹/₂	cup oil
1	teaspoon vanilla extract
	Grated peel of 1 lemon
2	pounds walnuts, ground
1¹/₂	cups hot milk
1¹/₂	cups sugar
2	tablespoons rum extract
3	egg whites

Dissolve the yeast and 1 tablespoon of the sugar in the warm milk in a bowl. Stir in 1 cup of the flour. Let stand for 15 minutes to rise. Beat the remaining 7 tablespoons sugar, egg, egg yolks, butter, oil, vanilla and lemon peel in a large bowl. Stir in the yeast mixture. Add the remaining flour gradually, mixing until a soft dough forms. Place in a greased bowl, turning to coat the surface. Let rise, covered, in a warm place until doubled in bulk. Combine the ground walnuts, hot milk, 1¹/₂ cups sugar and rum extract in a medium bowl. Beat the egg whites in a mixer bowl until soft peaks form. Fold into the walnut mixture. Punch down the dough. Roll ¹/₂ inch thick on a lightly floured surface. Spread the walnut mixture over the center of the dough. Roll up to enclose the filling. Place on a lightly greased baking sheet. Let rise, covered, for 30 minutes. Bake at 300 degrees for 50 to 60 minutes or until golden brown and the loaf tests done. Cool in the pan on a wire rack.

Yield: 1 loaf

Mary Tomacic, Croatian Women's Organization, Branch 1, Chicago, Illinois

CHAPTER Six

DESSERTS

A SEASON
of
CELEBRATING

New Year's Day

Japanese New Year

New Year's Day, Oshogatsu, is Japan's most important holiday. Families and friends gather and celebrate with an elaborate three-day feast. A traditional breakfast of rice cake and vegetable soup is served on New Year's morning amid wishes for good health and prosperity, a tradition enjoyed by all!

Chinese New Year

Good wishes and thanks for a safe and happy year are passed along to all on the Chinese New Year (held on the first day of the new moon between January 21 and February 20). In celebration of the New Year, everyone dresses in their finest clothes and is treated to a new pair of shoes. Friends exchange red greeting cards and children are given tangerines, oranges, and small red envelopes filled with coins. To bring good luck to the New Year, families eat special vegetables during a traditional luncheon. The celebration comes to an end on the day of the first full moon. The Great Dragon, the Chinese symbol of strength and goodness, leads a parade during the great Feast of Lanterns.

ARMENIAN CHRISTMAS PUDDING

1 cup husked whole
  wheat berries

3 quarts water

1¹/₂ cups dried apricots, cut
  into quarters

1¹/₂ cups golden raisins

2 cups sugar

2 tablespoons rose water

Rinse the wheat well. Place in a 5-quart saucepan with 3 quarts water. Bring to a boil; remove from the heat. Let stand, covered, for 8 to 10 hours. Simmer over low heat for 1¹/₂ hours. Rinse the apricots and raisins and add to the wheat mixture. Add the sugar. Simmer for 30 minutes; remove from the heat. Stir in the rose water. Spoon into a deep serving dish and garnish with walnuts and blanched almonds. Chill and serve cold.

Yield: 8 to 10 servings

Renee Berian, Armenian Youth Federation

DESSERTS

African American

BREAD PUDDING WITH APPLE-RAISIN SAUCE

10 slices whole wheat
  bread

1 whole egg

3 egg whites

1¹/₂ cups milk

¹/₄ cup sugar

¹/₄ cup packed brown
  sugar

1 teaspoon vanilla
  extract

¹/₂ teaspoon cinnamon

¹/₄ teaspoon nutmeg

¹/₄ teaspoon cloves

2 teaspoons sugar
  Apple-Raisin Sauce
  (at right)

Arrange the bread in overlapping slices in an 8-inch-square baking dish sprayed with nonstick cooking spray. Beat the egg, egg whites, milk, ¹/₄ cup sugar, brown sugar and vanilla in a mixer bowl until frothy. Pour over the bread. Sprinkle with a mixture of the cinnamon, nutmeg, cloves and 2 teaspoons sugar. Bake at 350 degrees for 30 to 35 minutes or until lightly browned and firm. Serve warm with warm Apple-Raisin Sauce.

Yield: 9 servings

Angela Cole

DESSERTS

BLUEBERRY PUDDING

This traditional Lakota (Sioux) dessert is a delicious finish to a festive meal.

2	**cups fresh or frozen blueberries**
¹/₂	**cup sugar**
4	**cups water**
2	**tablespoons (heaping) cornstarch**
¹/₂	**cup water**

Combine the blueberries, sugar and 4 cups water in a large saucepan. Bring to a boil over medium heat. Cook for 10 minutes, stirring occasionally. Mix the cornstarch with ¹/₂ cup water. Add to the blueberry mixture gradually until the mixture thickens. Cook over low heat for 5 minutes longer. Let cool before serving.

Yield: 4 servings

Julia Brown Wolf, Lakota (Sioux), Native American Tree Committee

Israel

CARROT PUDDING

1¹/₄	**cups sifted flour**
1	**teaspoon baking powder**
¹/₂	**teaspoon salt**
¹/₂	**teaspoon cinnamon**
¹/₂	**teaspoon nutmeg**
1	**cup grated carrots (about 6 carrots)**
1	**cup vegetable oil**
1	**egg, beaten**
¹/₂	**cup packed brown sugar**
2	**teaspoons lemon juice**
1	**teaspoon grated lemon peel**

Combine the flour, baking powder, salt, cinnamon and nutmeg in a bowl. Mix the carrots, oil, egg, brown sugar, lemon juice and lemon peel in a large bowl. Add the dry ingredients, mixing well. Pour into a greased 9-inch tube pan. Bake at 350 degrees for 45 minutes. Cool slightly; invert onto a serving plate. Serve hot.

Yield: 6 to 8 servings

Judy Kupfer

CITRON FROMAGE *Denmark*
LEMON BAVARIAN DESSERT

A favorite party dessert in Denmark.

1 tablespoon (heaping) plain gelatin

¹/₄ cup cold water

1 cup boiling water

4 egg yolks

1¹/₄ cups sugar

Juice and grated peel of 2 lemons

¹/₂ cup whipping cream

4 egg whites

Soften the gelatin in the cold water in a small bowl for 5 minutes. Add the boiling water, stirring until the gelatin is dissolved. Beat the egg yolks with the sugar in a mixer bowl until thick and pale yellow. Stir in the gelatin mixture slowly. Add the lemon juice and lemon peel. Cool until slightly congealed. Beat the cream in a small mixer bowl until stiff peaks form. Fold into the lemon mixture. Beat the egg whites in a medium mixer bowl until stiff peaks form. Fold into the lemon mixture. Spoon into a serving bowl. Chill before serving.

Yield: 4 to 6 servings
Karen Aagaard

CHRISTMAS DINNER IN DENMARK TRADITIONALLY BEGINS UPON THE FAMILY'S RETURN HOME FROM CHURCH ON JULEAFTEN, OR CHRISTMAS EVE.

SPANGUOLIU KISIELIUS *Lithuania*
CRANBERRY PUDDING

2 cups cranberries

5 cups water

1 cup sugar

2 tablespoons potato starch

2 teaspoons water

Rinse the cranberries. Combine with 5 cups water in a large saucepan. Bring to a boil. Cook for 7 minutes. Press through a sieve. Mix the sugar into the strained juice in a saucepan. Dissolve the potato starch in 2 teaspoons water. Stir into the juice. Bring to a boil. Cook for 3 minutes; cool. Serve in a glass serving dish to show off the bright color.

Yield: 4 to 6 servings
Lydia Ringus, Knights of Lithuanian Dancers

DESSERTS

In Finland, Riisipuuro (Rice Pudding) is made by bringing ³/₄ cup long grain rice and 2 quarts water to a boil in a large saucepan. Cook until the rice is very tender. Stir in milk until of desired consistency. Add 1 teaspoon salt. Simmer until thickened, stirring frequently. Sprinkle with sugar, cinnamon and half-and-half to serve, or serve with Fruitsoup (page 131).

Yield: 6 to 8 servings

Eeva Kallio, Finnladies of Chicagoland

Pudding "Chômeur" *Canada*

MAPLE SYRUP PUDDING CAKE

1¹/₂ cups maple syrup
³/₄   cup water
2   teaspoons butter
1   cup flour
1¹/₂ teaspoons baking powder
¹/₂   teaspoon salt
1   tablespoon shortening
¹/₂   cup sugar
1   egg, beaten
¹/₃   cup milk

Bring the maple syrup and water to a boil in a saucepan; remove from the heat. Stir in the butter; set aside. Combine the flour, baking powder and salt in a bowl. Cream the shortening and sugar in a mixer bowl until light and fluffy. Add the egg, mixing well. Fold in the dry ingredients alternately with the milk, beating well after each addition. Spread the batter in a greased 8-inch-square pan. Pour the maple syrup sauce evenly over the batter. Bake at 350 degrees for 35 minutes. Serve warm with plain or whipped cream.

Yield: 6 servings
The Canadian Women's Club of Chicago

African American

SWEET POTATO CUSTARD

1   cup mashed cooked sweet potato
¹/₂   cup mashed bananas (about 2 small bananas)
1   cup evaporated milk
2   tablespoons packed brown sugar
2   egg yolks, beaten
¹/₂   teaspoon salt
¹/₄   cup raisins
1   tablespoon sugar
1   teaspoon cinnamon

Mix the sweet potato and bananas in a medium bowl. Stir in the evaporated milk until smooth. Add the brown sugar, egg yolks and salt. Spoon into a 1-quart baking dish sprayed with non-stick cooking spray. Toss the raisins with sugar and cinnamon in a small bowl. Sprinkle over the sweet potato mixture. Bake at 300 degrees for 45 to 50 minutes or until a knife inserted near the center comes out clean. May use ¹/₃ cup egg substitute instead of the egg yolks.

Yield: 6 servings
Angela Cole

DESSERTS

Germany

RUM PUDDING

2 tablespoons unflavored gelatin

$^1/_2$ cup cold water

$3^1/_2$ cups boiling water

6 egg yolks

$^3/_4$ cup sugar

1 cup white rum

3 cups heavy cream, whipped

1 (10-ounce) package frozen raspberries, thawed

$^1/_2$ cup sugar

Soften the gelatin in cold water in a bowl. Add boiling water, stirring until the gelatin is dissolved. Let stand to cool. Beat the egg yolks with $^3/_4$ cup sugar in a mixer bowl until thick and pale yellow. Stir in the gelatin mixture gradually. Add the rum. Fold in the whipped cream. Pour into a serving dish; chill. Bring the raspberries and $^1/_2$ cup sugar to a boil in a saucepan. Cook for 5 minutes. Press through a sieve to strain; chill. Pour over the pudding to serve. Garnish with whipped cream.

Yield: 6 servings

Maria Bappert, Society of the Danube Swabians

Luxembourg

LEESCH CHRISTMAS PUDDING

1 cup sweet beef suet

1 cup thick cream or sour cream

1 egg, beaten

1 cup packed brown sugar

1 cup graham flour

$1^1/_2$ teaspoons baking soda

1 cup white flour

$1^1/_2$ cups chopped dates

1 cup chopped walnuts

$1^1/_2$ teaspoons flour

$^1/_2$ cup sugar

1 cup water

1 tablespoon butter

Rum or brandy to taste

Combine the finely chopped beef suet, cream, egg and brown sugar in a bowl; mix well. Sift the graham flour with the baking soda. Add the graham flour and 1 cup white flour to the suet mixture, stirring well. Fold in the dates and walnuts. Spoon into greased 1-pound cans; cover with waxed paper, tying to secure. Place in a pan of water in a 250-degree oven. Steam for $2^1/_2$ hours. Mix $1^1/_2$ teaspoons flour with sugar and water in a saucepan. Bring to a boil. Cook until thickened. Add butter and rum. Unmold the puddings onto serving plates. Drizzle with the rum sauce and serve warm.

Yield: 4 to 8 servings

Jean Weyrich

LEESCH CHRISTMAS PUDDING IS A VERY OLD RECIPE FROM THE LEESCH FAMILY, WHO EMIGRATED TO THE UNITED STATES IN 1888, FIRST TO CHENOA, ILLINOIS, AND LATER TO REDFIELD, SOUTH DAKOTA, WHERE THE OLDEST MEMBER OF THE FAMILY CELEBRATED HER 99TH BIRTHDAY. THIS PUDDING HAS ALWAYS BEEN A PART OF CHRISTMAS CELEBRATIONS. IT MAY BE MADE AHEAD OF TIME AND STORED IN THE REFRIGERATOR OR FREEZER, BUT WARM IT THOROUGHLY BEFORE SERVING.

DESSERTS

Guatemala

CHRISTMAS PLUM PUDDING

1 cup each raisins and
   currants

$^1/_2$ cup citron, minced

2 cups flour

4 eggs, beaten

1 cup (heaping) sugar

1 teaspoon ground cloves

2 teaspoons cinnamon

$^1/_2$ teaspoon nutmeg

1 teaspoon salt

1 cup milk

1 cup blanched almonds

2 cups fine bread crumbs

1 cup beef suet, minced

1 teaspoon baking soda

1 tablespoon warm water

Coat the raisins, currants and citron with a small amount of the flour; set aside. Beat the eggs with the sugar, cloves, cinnamon, nutmeg, salt and milk in a bowl. Add the fruit, chopped almonds, bread crumbs and suet. Dissolve the baking soda in warm water. Add to the mixture with the remaining flour, mixing well. Spoon into greased 1-pound tins; cover tightly. Place in a large saucepan half filled with water. Steam, tightly covered, over low heat for 4 hours. Unmold onto serving plates. Serve with a lemon or hard sauce.

Yield: 4 to 6 servings

Consulate General of Guatemala

SLIZIKAI SU AGUONU PIENU *Lithuania*

CHRISTMAS EVE BISCUITS

2 envelopes active dry
   yeast

2 cups warm milk

$^1/_2$ cup sugar

4 cups flour

$^1/_2$ cup vegetable oil

$^1/_2$ cup poppy seed pie
   filling

   Poppy Seed Milk
   (page 12)

Dissolve the yeast in the warm milk with sugar in a bowl. Let stand in a warm place for 20 minutes. Mix the flour, yeast mixture, oil and poppy seed filling in a large bowl until the dough forms a soft ball. Let rise, covered, in a warm place until doubled in bulk. Knead gently for 2 to 3 minutes. Roll small portions into $^1/_2$-inch-thick ropes. Cut into 1-inch lengths. Place on a floured cookie sheet. Bake at 350 degrees for 8 to 10 minutes or until golden brown. Cool in a deep, flat serving dish. Pour warm Poppy Seed Milk over the cookies.

Yield: 20 to 24 servings

Lydia Ringus, Knights of Lithuanian Dancers

Ireland

GUINESS CAKE

1 bottle Guiness stout beer

4 eggs, well beaten

1 1/2 cups butter, softened

3/4 pound brown sugar

4 cups flour

1 teaspoon baking soda

1 pound raisins

1 pound currants

1/2 cup mixed minced citrus peel

Heat the stout in a small saucepan until lukewarm. Pour over the beaten eggs in a bowl, mixing well. Cream the butter and brown sugar in a mixer bowl until light and fluffy. Mix the flour and baking soda together. Add to the creamed mixture alternately with the stout mixture, beating well after each addition. Fold in the raisins, currants and citrus peel. Pour into a large greased tube pan. Bake at 300 degrees for 3 hours. Place a pan of water in the oven while baking to moisten the cake.

Yield: 16 servings
Mary Griffin, Irish American Heritage Center

Israel

HONEY CAKE

3 1/2 cups sifted flour

1/4 teaspoon salt

1 1/2 teaspoons baking powder

1 teaspoon baking soda

1/2 teaspoon cinnamon

1/4 teaspoon nutmeg

1/8 teaspoon ground cloves

1/2 teaspoon ginger

4 eggs

3/4 cup sugar

4 teaspoons vegetable oil

2 cups dark honey

1/2 cup brewed coffee

1 1/2 cups walnuts or almonds, chopped

Sift the flour, salt, baking powder, baking soda, cinnamon, nutmeg, cloves and ginger into a large bowl. Beat the eggs in a mixer bowl. Add the sugar gradually, beating until thick and pale yellow. Add the oil, honey and coffee, beating well. Fold in the flour mixture and the walnuts. Grease an 11x16-inch baking pan and line with foil. Pour in the batter. Bake at 325 degrees for 1 1/4 hours, or until browned and the cake tests done. Cool in the pan on a wire rack. Remove from the pan to a serving plate. May use two 9-inch loaf pans and bake for 50 minutes.

Yield: 15 servings
Embassy of Israel and Consulate General of Israel to the Midwest

DESERTS

HONEY CAKE IS A MUST FOR ROSH HASHANA, THE JEWISH NEW YEAR, SINCE ITS SWEETNESS SYMBOLIZES THE WISHES FOR A GOOD YEAR AHEAD.

DESSERTS

FRUIT COMPOTE IS A
TRADITIONAL DESSERT SERVED
AT CHRISTMAS IN MANY
COUNTRIES. THE FOLLOWING
RECIPES FROM POLAND,
HUNGARY, LITHUANIA,
BELARUS, UKRAINE, FINLAND
AND THE NETHERLANDS
INDICATE THE VARIETY OF WAYS
THE FRUIT IS PREPARED. ONE
OF THE MOST ELABORATE
FRUIT COMPOTES IS FROM
POLAND, WHERE THE
CHRISTMAS MEAL IS
MEATLESS.

Poland
TWELVE-FRUIT COMPOTE

3	cups water
1	pound mixed dried fruits (pears, figs, apricots and peaches)
1	cup pitted prunes
1/2	cup raisins or currants
1	cup pitted sweet cherries
2	apples, peeled and sliced, or 6 ounces dried apple slices
1/3	cup cranberries
1	cup sugar
1	lemon, sliced
6	whole cloves
2	cinnamon sticks
1	orange
1/3	cup grapes, pomegranate seeds or pitted plums
1/2	cup fruit-flavored brandy

Combine the water, the mixed dried fruits, prunes and raisins in a 6-quart kettle. Bring to a boil. Simmer, covered, for 20 minutes or until the fruit is plumped. Add the cherries, apple slices and cranberries. Stir in sugar, lemon, cloves and cinnamon sticks. Grate the peel from the orange and set aside. Section the orange, removing skin and discarding the white membrane. Add to the fruit mixture. Stir in the grapes and the brandy. Bring to a boil; remove from the heat. Stir in the orange peel. Let stand, covered, for 15 minutes.

Yield: 12 servings
Polish Scouting Organization, Z.H.P.—Inc.

Lithuania

KOMPOTAS

In Lithuania, the compote dish is called *Kompotas*. To prepare, combine 10 cups of water, 1 cup of sugar and 2 pounds of assorted dried fruits in a large kettle. Simmer for 15 minutes. Add 1 chopped lemon, the grated peel of an orange, 3 whole cloves and 1 cinnamon stick. Simmer for 5 minutes longer and remove from the heat. Stir in $^1/_2$ cup of fruit-flavored liqueur and prunes. Let stand to cool slightly and serve warm.

Belarus

KAMPOT Z FRUCHTAU

The *Kampot z Fruchtau* from Belarus omits cinnamon and cloves, but they may be added for flavor. Simmer 1 to 2 pounds of dried mixed fruits, such as prunes, apricots, apples, raisins, pears, figs or peaches with enough water to cover (about 2 cups of water for each 1 pound of fruit). Bring the mixture to a boil, then reduce the heat and simmer until the fruit is tender. Lemon or orange peel may also be added, and sugar or honey for sweetness.

Finland

FRUITSOUP

In Finland, the dried fruit dessert is called *Sekahedelmäkeitto*, or Fruitsoup. One pound of mixed dried fruits is simmered in $2^1/_2$ quarts of water with 1 cinnamon stick and 1 cup of sugar for 1 hour. To thicken the mixture, mix 2 tablespoons of potato starch with 2 tablespoons of cold water. Bring the fruit mixture to a boil and stir in the potato starch mixture. Remove the fruit from the heat and let stand to cool. Serve over rice pudding or drizzle with half-and-half. Traditionally an almond is hidden in the rice, which is said to bring good luck to the person who finds it.

The Netherlands

KRENTJEBREI

Krentjebrei is the name of this holiday dish when served in The Netherlands. Bring $2^1/_2$ quarts of water to a boil. Stir in $^1/_2$ cup of barley and boil the mixture until the barley is tender. Add 1 cup raisins and simmer for 15 minutes. Add 1 cup currants, $^1/_4$ cup cider vinegar, 1 tablespoon port wine and a 1-quart bottle of bessensap, or substitute a 3-ounce package of rasp-berry gelatin. Simmer for 5 to 10 minutes. Serve the dessert warm or cold.

DESSERTS

A WARMED FRUIT COMPOTE BEGINS MANY SPECIAL-OCCASION MEALS IN HUNGARY. FOR A QUICK RECIPE, USE COMMERCIALLY PACKAGED AND PREPARED DRIED FRUIT AND BOIL IT UNTIL TENDER. ADD SUGAR TO TASTE, WHICH FOR HUNGARIANS IS MERELY A SPRINKLE, SINCE THEY PREFER THE TART FLAVOR. SERVE THE COMPOTE WARM.

—⁂—

THE UKRAINIAN UZVAR IS PREPARED IN MUCH THE SAME WAY AS IN HUNGARY, USING 1 TO 2 POUNDS OF DRIED MIXED FRUIT, WATER, 1 CINNAMON STICK, 6 CLOVES, AND HONEY OR SUGAR TO TASTE. LEMON PEEL MAY BE ADDED FOR ADDITIONAL FLAVOR.

DESSERTS

It is a tradition in Greece that the Christmas tree is decorated the day before Christmas with gifts for the children. The presents remain there until New Year's Eve, when they finally can be opened.

PLUM CAKE

5	eggs
1³/₄	cups sugar
2	cups oil
¹/₂	teaspoon baking powder
2¹/₃	cups flour
12	blue plums, cut into halves

Beat the eggs, sugar and oil in a mixer bowl until thick and pale yellow. Add the baking powder and flour, mixing well. Pour half of the batter into a 9x12-inch cake pan. Arrange the plum halves over the batter. Cover with the remaining batter. Bake at 300 degrees for 45 to 50 minutes or until the cake tests done. Serve sprinkled with confectioners' sugar.

Yield: 12 servings

Vala Vakselis, Bielarusian Coordinating Committee of Chicago

WALNUT CAKE

This dessert, made for the holidays and all festive occasions, is served as a special treat after the meal.

²/₃	cup butter, softened
²/₃	cup sugar
3	egg yolks
1	teaspoon vanilla extract
³/₄	cup farina
1	teaspoon cinnamon
1	cup chopped walnuts
3	egg whites
¹/₃	cup sugar
¹/₃	cup water

Cream the butter with ²/₃ cup of the sugar. Add the egg yolks and vanilla, beating until light and fluffy. Add the farina and cinnamon alternately with the walnuts, stirring well. Beat the egg whites in a mixer bowl until soft peaks form. Fold the egg whites into the batter gently until well blended. Pour into a buttered 9-inch-square cake pan. Bake at 375 degrees for 35 minutes or until the cake tests done. Mix the remaining ¹/₃ cup sugar with the water in a saucepan. Bring to a boil. Cook until slightly thickened. Pour over the warm cake. Cool in the pan on a wire rack. Cut into squares or diamond shapes to serve.

Yield: 12 servings

Sophie Liambotis, Peiraikon Hellenic School

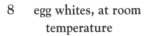

Romania

CHOCOLATE MERINGUE TORTE

8   **egg whites, at room temperature**

$^1/_2$ **teaspoon cream of tartar**

$1^3/_4$ **cups sugar**

1   **teaspoon vanilla extract**

Cocoa Cream

2   **cups milk**

$1^1/_2$ **tablespoons baking cocoa**

$^1/_4$ **cup sugar**

     Pinch of salt

3   **tablespoons flour**

6   **ounces whipped butter, at room temperature**

     Rum to taste

Beat the egg whites and cream of tartar in a mixer bowl at medium speed until soft peaks form. Sprinkle in $1^3/_4$ cups sugar 2 tablespoons at a time, beating continuously until the sugar is dissolved (about 15 minutes). Add the vanilla. Beat at high speed until stiff, glossy peaks form. Line 2 baking sheets with waxed paper. Trace four 8-inch circles. Spread the meringue in the circles to a $^1/_2$-inch thickness, making 4 layers. Bake at 250 degrees for 45 minutes. Turn off the oven. Leave the meringues in the oven for 8 to 10 hours to dry. Wrap tightly when dried and cooled to prevent moisture entering that will soften them. To make cocoa cream, bring the milk to a boil in a saucepan; remove from the heat. Combine the cocoa, $^1/_4$ cup sugar, salt and flour. Add to the hot milk, whisking until smooth. Cook over low heat until the mixture begins to boil and thicken, stirring vigorously. Turn into a bowl and place bowl in ice to cool; continue stirring. Whip the butter in a medium mixer bowl until light and fluffy. Add the cocoa mixture gradually, beating constantly. Stir in rum; let stand to cool slightly. Spread the cocoa mixture over each of the meringue layers. Stack the layers and frost the side. Garnish with shaved chocolate and whipped cream. Frost no more than 1 hour before serving to avoid softening the meringue.

Yield: 10 servings

The Romanian Christmas Group Holy Nativity

DESSERTS

THE LEGENDARY "ENGADINER NUSSTORTE" HAS DEFINITELY MADE A BIG CONTRIBUTION TO THE FAME OF MANY BAKERS IN GRAUBUENDEN, SWITZERLAND, WHERE THE RECIPES ARE HANDED DOWN FROM ONE GENERATION TO THE NEXT.

PECAN PIES

1³/4 cups sugar

¹/4 cup whipping cream

¹/3 cup honey

1³/4 cups chopped pecans

2³/4 cups flour

1 cup sugar

1¹/4 cups butter, softened

2 eggs, beaten

2 egg yolks

Pinch of salt

Grated peel of ¹/2 lemon

Cook 1³/4 cups sugar in a nonstick saucepan until it melts and begins to caramelize. Add the whipping cream. Bring to a boil. Stir in the honey and pecans; remove from the heat. Let stand to cool slightly. Combine the flour, 1 cup sugar and butter in a bowl, mixing until the dough is crumbly. Add the eggs, 1 of the egg yolks, salt and lemon peel. Mix well. Remove ²/3 of the pastry and separate into 2 equal portions; roll out on a floured surface. Place in 2 buttered 8-inch round pie pans. Pour equal amounts of the pecan mixture into the prepared pans. Divide the remaining dough into 2 portions. Roll out and cover the pecan fillings. Decorate the top pastry if desired. Brush with the remaining egg yolk. Bake at 400 degrees for 25 minutes. Let stand for 24 hours before serving.

Yield: 16 servings
Swiss Club of Chicago

Luxembourg

PLUM PIE WITH OLD-FASHIONED YEAST CRUST

1	envelope active dry yeast
2	tablespoons warm water
3	tablespoons sugar
1/4	teaspoon salt
1/3	cup lukewarm milk
1 1/2	cups flour
1	egg
3	tablespoons lukewarm melted butter
30	ripe medium Italian plums
3	to 4 tablespoons sugar

Dissolve the yeast in warm water in a large bowl. Let stand for 2 to 3 minutes. Add 3 tablespoons sugar, salt, milk and 1/2 cup of the flour. Beat for 2 minutes. Add the egg and butter. Beat until smooth. Add enough of the remaining flour to make a soft dough. Let rise, covered, in a warm place until doubled in bulk. Knead on a floured surface until smooth. Roll out into a 12-inch circle, 1/4 inch thick. Place in a buttered 10-inch pie plate. Trim and flute the edge. Let rise for 30 minutes. Cut the plums along the seam and remove the pits. Cut an "X" halfway through each half and fold back to form 4 peaks. Arrange overlapping rows of the plums peel side down, beginning at the outer edge of the pie plate. Bake at 350 degrees for 30 minutes or until browned and bubbly. Sprinkle with 3 to 4 tablespoons sugar.

Yield: 6 servings
Madeleine Thomé

THIS RECIPE FROM LUXEMBOURG MAY ALSO BE PREPARED USING APRICOTS, RHUBARB OR APPLES FOR THE FILLING. IF FILLING WITH PLUMS AND THEY ARE UNDERRIPE, PLACE THEM IN A GLASS BOWL AND SPRINKLE WITH 2 TABLESPOONS SUGAR. MICROWAVE ON HIGH FOR 2 TO 3 MINUTES.

TARTE AU SUCRE *Canada*

SUGAR PIE

2	cups packed light brown sugar
1	tablespoon flour
1/2	cup (15%) cream
1/2	cup milk
2	teaspoons butter
1	(9-inch) unbaked pie shell

Combine the brown sugar, flour, cream, milk and butter in a saucepan. Bring to a boil. Cook for 2 to 2 1/2 minutes, stirring constantly. Pour into the pie shell. Bake on the bottom oven rack at 450 degrees for 15 minutes or until the crust is golden. Serve with vanilla ice cream.

Yield: 6 servings
The Canadian Women's Club of Chicago

Desserts

Goa, a coastal state in southwestern India, is the source of this recipe. Goa was a Portuguese territory for more than 400 years before it became a part of India in the 1960s. This recipe is similar to those found in Portugal and Brazil. Traditionally, bibinça was made on an outdoor stone stove fired by coal. Because this was such a hot, tedious and long process, bibinça was only made for special occasions. Today, it is a breeze to make it; however, it is not for the cholesterol conscious!

India
BIBINÇA

4   to 4¹/₂ cups cake flour
4   (15-ounce) cans sweetened cream of coconut
40   egg yolks
4   cups sugar
2   teaspoons cardamom seeds, finely ground
1¹/₂ cups clarified butter

Combine the flour and coconut cream in a large bowl. Beat in the egg yolks, sugar and cardamom. Brush a deep baking pan with the butter. Pour in 1 cup of the batter. Bake at 300 degrees for 10 to 15 minutes or until light brown. Brush with 3 tablespoons of the butter. Pour in 1 cup of the batter. Broil at 300 to 325 degrees for 15 minutes or until browned. Repeat the process until all the batter is used, brushing each layer with butter before adding more batter. There will be from 7 to 12 layers. Cut in ¹/₄-inch slices and serve warm. Store in the refrigerator.

Yield: 12 to 15 servings

Pat Paprocki, India Catholic Association of America

Rava Ladu *India*
SWEET RAISIN-CASHEW BALLS

¹/₄ cup chopped cashews
¹/₄ cup raisins
¹/₄ cup melted butter or oil
2   cups Rava (cream of wheat), prepared
1   cup sugar
¹/₂ teaspoon cardamom powder
¹/₄ cup hot milk

Stir-fry the cashews and raisins in a small amount of the butter in a skillet for 2 to 3 minutes. Remove and set aside; wipe out the skillet. Fry the cream of wheat in the remaining butter in the skillet over low heat. Stir in the sugar and cardamom powder. Remove from the heat. Add the milk, stirring until smooth. Fold in the cashews and raisins. Shape the mixture into small balls.

Yield: 32 servings

Lucy Menezes, India Catholic Association of America

DESSERTS

TABLATA *Belize*
COCONUT CANDY

2   **medium coconuts**

1³/₄ **cups packed brown
     sugar**

Break open the coconuts. Drain and reserve the liquid. Grate the meat. Combine the liquid, coconut meat and brown sugar in a heavy iron saucepan. Cook over medium to low heat for 45 minutes or until the mixture begins to hold together. May add evaporated milk for desired consistency and minced ginger for flavor. Cook for 5 minutes longer. Pour the mixture onto a greased board or baking sheet. Let stand until cool and hardened. Cut into small pieces.

Yield: 15 servings

Mrs. A. MacFarlane, Belizean Cultural Association

MARZIPAN *Denmark*
ALMOND PASTE CANDY

A favorite candy, the dough can be shaped to resemble fruit or vegetables, and painted with a paste made from food coloring and confectioners' sugar.

1   **cup prepared almond
     paste**

2   **egg whites**

1   **(1-pound) package
     confectioners' sugar,
     sifted**

¹/₂ **teaspoon vanilla
     extract**

¹/₂ **teaspoon almond
     extract**

Combine the almond paste and egg whites in a bowl. Beat for 3 minutes. Add the confectioners' sugar, vanilla and almond extracts. Beat for 5 minutes longer. Chill the mixture, covered, for 8 to 10 hours before proceeding. Shape the dough into a ⁷/₈-inch thick log. Slice into equal portions. Shape into balls for apples, oranges or tomatoes, or elongate and shape as bananas or point one end for carrots and radishes. Paint the marzipan fruit with diluted color paste, or add food coloring to the dough before shaping.

Yield: 25 to 30 servings

*Carol Bach, Danish Sisterhood Society,
Olga Lodge 11*

DESSERTS

In Japan, tree-decorating is celebrated on July 7. The event is called "Tanabata" (which means "July 7"), and bamboo trees are decorated with origami ornaments.

KUROMAME *Japan*

SWEET BLACK BEANS

1   (12-ounce) package kuromame (dried black beans)
³/₄ cup honey
³/₄ cup sugar
    Peel of 1 orange, thinly sliced
    Peel of 1 lemon, thinly sliced
1³/₄ teaspoons salt
1³/₄ tablespoons soy sauce

Rinse the kuromame; soak for 10 to 12 hours. Drain and rinse well. Place in a pressure cooker with water to cover. Bring to a boil, skimming off foam. Pour off some of the water, leaving just enough to cover the beans. Cover tightly. Bring to a boil. Cook until the steam begins to escape from the pressure opening. Attach the pressure gauge; lower the heat. Cook for 30 minutes. Remove from the heat and allow pressure to fall before removing gauge or cover. Drain the beans and return to the cooker. Add the honey, sugar, orange and lemon peel and salt. Simmer for 10 minutes. Remove from the heat and let cool for 5 minutes. Stir in the soy sauce.

Yield: 6 to 8 servings
Tampopo-Kai

MOCHIKO *Japan*

CHEWY RICE CONFECTION

1   cup water
¹/₄ stick pink or white agar agar (kanten or Japanese gelatin)
²/₃ cup sugar
1   cup mochiko (sweet rice powder)
    Katakuriko (potato starch powder)

Line a 9-inch-square pan with plastic wrap and set aside. Line a wooden steamer or rice cooker with a towel and set aside. Bring the water to a boil in a saucepan over medium heat. Add the agar agar, sugar and mochiko. Cook until dissolved, stirring constantly. Pour into the prepared steamer. Steam for 1 hour or until the mixture is puffy. Place in a heavy bowl, scraping the mixture off the cloth. Pound with a mallet for 5 minutes, turning frequently. The mixture will be sticky but chewy. Place in the prepared pan; let cool. Cut into 3-inch squares. Dust each square with the potato starch to prevent the pieces from sticking to each other.

Yield: 9 servings
Roy Okamoto

ÄIDIN ÄSSÄT *Finland*

MOTHER'S "S" COOKIES

10	tablespoons butter or margarine, softened
1	cup sugar
3	eggs
1	teaspoon cinnamon
1	teaspoon baking powder
2¹/₂	cups flour
	Cinnamon and sugar mixture

Cream the butter and sugar in a mixer bowl until light and fluffy. Add the eggs, beating well. Combine the cinnamon, baking powder and flour. Stir into the creamed mixture. Shape into a long rope ¹/₂ inch thick. Cut into 3-inch lengths. Roll in a mixture of cinnamon and sugar; shape into an "S." Bake on a greased cookie sheet at 375 degrees for 10 minutes or until golden brown.

Yield: 30 to 40 cookies

Eeva Kallio, Finnladies of Chicagoland

DESSERTS

A FINNISH CHRISTMAS WOULD NOT HAVE BEEN COMPLETE WITHOUT MOTHER'S "S" COOKIES. THEY ARE FAIRLY INEXPENSIVE TO MAKE AND THE INGREDIENTS ARE USUALLY ON HAND. EEVA KALLIO CONTINUES TO MAKE THESE FOR THE HOLIDAYS.

BIBBI'S BRUNA KAKOR *Sweden*

BROWN COOKIES

1	cup sugar
2	teaspoons baking soda
2¹/₃	cups flour
1	teaspoon dark corn syrup
1	cup less 1 tablespoon butter, softened

Combine the sugar, baking soda and flour in a bowl. Add the corn syrup and cut in the butter until crumbly. Knead until the mixture holds together, but do not overwork the dough. Shape into 3 long logs. Place on a cookie sheet; flatten slightly. Bake at 300 degrees for 20 to 30 minutes or until golden brown and cracks form on top. Remove from the oven. Slice the logs diagonally into bars.

Yield: 30 to 40 cookies

Birgit Swanson, Linnea South Suburban Swedish Women's Club

DESSERTS

CHRISTMAS COOKIES

1	cup melted butter, cooled
$^1/_2$	cup warm water
1	teaspoon baking powder
1	tablespoon brandy
$^1/_4$	teaspoon grated orange peel
2	to 3 cups flour
$^1/_2$	to 1 cup chopped walnuts
	Heavy syrup
	Ground walnuts

Combine the butter, water, baking powder, brandy and orange peel in a bowl. Add the flour gradually, stirring until a soft dough forms. Shape into $2^1/_2$-inch-long rolls, 1 inch thick. Flatten the rolls on a wire strainer to make an impression of the wires. Fill the center with $^1/_2$ teaspoon of the chopped walnuts. Fold up the dough to enclose the walnuts. Place on a cookie sheet. Bake at 350 degrees for 25 minutes or until lightly browned. Cool on wire racks. Dip in heavy syrup and roll in ground walnuts.

Yield: 20 to 24 cookies

Renee Berian, Armenian Youth Federation

Scotland

EMPIRE BISCUITS

4	cups flour
1	cup sugar
2	cups butter, softened
2	eggs, beaten
1	cup sifted confectioners' sugar
1	tablespoon lemon juice
$^1/_2$	teaspoon vanilla extract or water
	Jam

Combine the flour and 1 cup sugar in a large bowl. Cut in the butter until the mixture is crumbly. Add the eggs, stirring until a soft dough forms. Roll the dough $^1/_4$ inch thick. Cut into circles with a cookie cutter. Bake on a greased cookie sheet at 450 degrees for 12 to 15 minutes. Cool on a wire rack. Beat the confectioners' sugar, lemon juice and vanilla in a small bowl until smooth. Spread jam over half of the cookies; top with the remaining cookies. Drizzle with the confectioners' sugar icing. Garnish with a cherry.

Yield: 30 to 40 cookies

Laurie Grant, Thistle & Heather Highland Dancers

KOLACKI *Lithuania*
CHEESE-FILLED BUTTER COOKIES

2 cups butter, softened
½ cup sugar
1 teaspoon vanilla extract
4 cups flour
2 tablespoons milk
1 cup dry cottage cheese
3 ounces cream cheese
1 egg yolk
1 teaspoon vanilla extract
Confectioners' sugar

Cream the butter and sugar in a mixer bowl until light and fluffy. Stir in 1 teaspoon vanilla. Add the flour and milk, stirring until dough forms a ball. Shape the dough into 1-inch balls, making an indentation in the center of each one. Place on a greased cookie sheet. Beat the cottage cheese, cream cheese, egg yolk and 1 teaspoon vanilla in a bowl. Beat in enough confectioners' sugar to thicken the mixture. Spoon a small amount of the mixture into the indentations. Bake at 325 degrees for 20 to 25 minutes. Cookies should not brown. Sprinkle with confectioners' sugar while hot.

Yield: 24 to 36 cookies
Carol Bart

KOURAMBIEDES *Greece*
POWDERED SUGAR COOKIES

2 cups unsalted butter, softened
2 egg yolks
1 cup confectioners' sugar
1 to 2 ounces anisette liqueur
1 cup finely chopped almonds (optional)
4 cups flour
1 tablespoon baking powder
Confectioners' sugar

Cream the butter in a mixer bowl for 40 minutes. Add the egg yolks, beating well. Stir in 1 cup confectioners' sugar, anisette and almonds. Sift the flour and baking powder together. Add to the creamed mixture, stirring well. Chill the dough until firm. Pinch off small pieces of the dough and shape into crescents. Place on a greased cookie sheet. Bake at 350 degrees for 10 to 12 minutes; cool on wire racks. Dust with confectioners' sugar.

Yield: 48 cookies
Alberta Kontos, Lansing Business Women's Association

DESSERTS

KOURAMBIEDES ARE TRADITIONALLY PREPARED FOR CHRISTMAS AND NEW YEAR'S DAY. FOR CHRISTMAS, EACH COOKIE IS STUDDED WITH A CLOVE TO SYMBOLIZE THE GIFT OF SPICES BROUGHT BY THE WISE MEN TO THE CHRIST CHILD.

———

TO MAKE ARMENIAN KURABIA (BUTTER COOKIES), CREAM 2 CUPS SOFTENED UNSALTED BUTTER IN A MIXER BOWL UNTIL LIGHT AND FLUFFY. ADD 2 CUPS CONFECTIONERS' SUGAR, BEATING WELL. STIR IN 3 CUPS FLOUR GRADUALLY UNTIL A SOFT DOUGH FORMS. ROLL OUT THE DOUGH AND CUT INTO DESIRED SHAPES. PLACE ON A GREASED COOKIE SHEET. BAKE AT 300 DEGREES FOR 20 MINUTES OR UNTIL LIGHTLY BROWNED.

YIELD: 36 COOKIES

RENEE BERIAN, ARMENIAN YOUTH FEDERATION

DESSERTS

HONEY CAKES ARE THE
FRAGRANT COOKIES THAT
HANG ON THE HUNGARIAN
CHRISTMAS TREE AT THE
MUSEUM OF SCIENCE AND
INDUSTRY. THE SPICES,
CINNAMON AND CLOVE, AND
THE BROWN SUGAR AND
HONEY GIVE OFF
A WONDERFUL SMELL.

LUSIKKA LEÍVÁT *Finland*
SPOON COOKIES

In Finland, coffee is commonly served to guests with seven sorts of
delicacies. These cookies are often one of the seven.

1	cup butter
1	cup (heaping) sugar
2½	cups flour
1	teaspoon baking soda
1	teaspoon vanilla extract
	Jam

Brown the butter in a small saucepan, being careful not to burn. Pour into a mixer bowl and let stand until cool. Add the sugar, beating well. Stir in the flour, baking soda and vanilla. Press the dough onto a teaspoon. Slide off onto a cookie sheet covered with parchment paper. Bake at 325 degrees for 15 minutes or until slightly browned. Spread half of the cookies with jam. Top with the remaining cookies. May chill the dough in the mixer bowl for 2 to 3 hours.

Yield: 15 to 20 cookies

Toni Laakso, Finnladies of Chicagoland

MÉZES KALÁCS *Hungary*
HONEY CAKES

¾	cup plus 2 tablespoons shortening
5	pounds rye flour
2¼	cups packed brown sugar
4	teaspoons baking soda
1	teaspoon ground cloves
4	to 5 teaspoons cinnamon
6	tablespoons lemon juice
5	to 6 eggs, beaten
1	(4-pound) jar honey

Cut the shortening into the flour in a large bowl until crumbly. Add the brown sugar, baking soda, cloves and cinnamon, mixing well. Stir in the lemon juice, eggs and honey to make a soft dough. Chill for 8 to 10 hours. Knead in additional flour on a lightly floured surface until the dough is no longer sticky. Roll the dough ¼-inch thick and cut out in desired shapes. Cut a small hole in each to hang on the tree. Place on a greased cookie sheet. Bake at 350 degrees for 8 to 10 minutes or longer if used for decorations. Cool and recut the holes. May frost with royal frosting that is made from meringue powder.

Yield: 100 cookies

Margaret Kun, Calvin Reformed Church of Lynwood, Illinois

MUSKACONE *Serbia*

WALNUT COOKIES

2 cups ground roasted walnuts

2 cups confectioners' sugar

2 eggs

2 egg whites

1/4 cup rum

2 to 3 cups graham cracker crumbs

Sugar

Combine the walnuts, confectioners' sugar, eggs, egg whites and rum in a bowl; mix well. Add the graham cracker crumbs gradually, stirring until the dough is stiff but pliable. Coat a cookie mold with sugar. Press dough into the mold and level off. Tap out onto a greased cookie sheet, leaving 1 1/2 inches between each cookie. Repeat with the remaining dough, coating the mold each time with sugar. May roll the dough into balls and coat with the sugar. Bake at 225 degrees for 1 hour.

Yield: 36 cookies

Miryana Trbuhovich, Federation of Circles of Serbian Sisters, Midwestern Metropolitanate of the Serbian Orthodox Church

DESSERTS

THIS RECIPE FOR WALNUT COOKIES HAS BEEN HANDED DOWN FROM MIRYANA TRBUHOVICH'S GRANDFATHER, A MASTER BAKER IN ZEMUN, SERBIA IN THE LATE 1800S, TO HER MOTHER, MRS. DANICA SIMICH. IT IS A TRADITIONAL COOKIE PRESSED FROM A COPPER MOLD SHAPED LIKE A BOW TIE, ALTHOUGH OTHER MOLDS MAY BE USED. MIRYANA USES HER MOTHER'S ORIGINAL COPPER MOLD.

Finland

OATMEAL COOKIES

Christina Newenhouse baked these cookies with her mother as a child, and continues to have them on hand at home for family and friends. They are easy and quick to make.

3 cups rolled oats

1/2 cup (scant) flour

15 tablespoons margarine or butter, melted

1 egg

2/3 cup sugar

1 teaspoon baking powder

1/4 teaspoon almond extract

Combine the oats and flour in a bowl. Add the melted margarine, stirring until moistened; let stand. Beat the egg and sugar in a mixer bowl until frothy. Stir in the baking powder and almond extract. Pour into the oat mixture, stirring well. Drop by teaspoonfuls onto a greased cookie sheet. Bake at 350 degrees for 8 to 12 minutes or until lightly browned around the edges.

Yield: 40 cookies

Christina Newenhouse, Finnladies of Chicagoland

DESSERTS

These gingersnap cookies are often hung on a specially painted red pepparkakor Christmas tree during the Festival of Light on December 13, St. Lucia's Day.

———

To make Rohlicky Crescents from the Czech Republic, cream 1/2 cup confectioners' sugar, 2 cups softened butter and 1 teaspoon vanilla extract in a mixer bowl until light and fluffy. Stir in 2 1/4 cups chopped walnuts. Add 4 cups flour and mix well. Shape the dough into small balls. Flatten slightly and shape into small crescents. Place on a greased cookie sheet. Bake at 300 degrees for 8 minutes or until light golden. Cool on a wire rack. Dust with additional confectioners' sugar. May refrigerate the dough for several days.

Yield: 48 cookies

Club Bedrich Smetana

MORMOR'S PEPPARKAKOR *Sweden*
SWEDISH GINGERSNAP COOKIES

1	cup butter, softened
1 1/2	cups sugar
1	tablespoon dark corn syrup
1	egg, beaten
3	cups flour, sifted
1 1/2	teaspoons baking soda
2 1/2	teaspoons cinnamon
2 1/2	teaspoons ginger
2 1/2	teaspoons ground cloves
	Extra-fine sugar

Cream the butter and sugar in a mixer bowl until light and fluffy. Beat in the corn syrup and egg. Add the flour, baking soda, cinnamon, ginger and cloves, stirring until a soft dough forms. Chill until firm. Roll the dough very thinly on a floured surface. Place on a greased cookie sheet and sprinkle with extra-fine sugar. Bake at 350 degrees for 15 minutes.

Yield: 36 cookies

Jaclen Cole, Linnea South Suburban Swedish Women's Club

Scotland
RAISIN SQUARES

2/3	cup shortening
1	teaspoon salt
2 1/4	cups flour
1 1/2	(15-ounce) packages seedless raisins
1/2	cup sugar
1	teaspoon lemon juice
1	tablespoon cornstarch or flour
	Sugar

Cut the shortening into a mixture of salt and flour in a bowl until crumbly. Add enough cold water to make a firm, pliable pastry. Divide into 2 equal portions. Roll each portion on a floured surface 1/4 inch thick. Line a greased cookie sheet with a 1/2-inch rim with 1 portion of the dough. Simmer the raisins in water to cover for 5 minutes; drain. Stir in 1/2 cup sugar, lemon juice, cornstarch and a small amount of water to make of desired consistency. Cool. Spread over the pastry. Cover with the remaining pastry. Brush with a mixture of sugar and water to glaze. Bake at 425 degrees for 30 minutes or until lightly browned. Cool on the cookie sheet on a wire rack. Sprinkle with confectioners' sugar and cut into squares to serve.

Yield: 36 squares

Pat LeNoble, Thistle & Heather Highland Dancers

MOLASSES COOKIES

³/₄ cup butter, softened

1 egg

¹/₂ cup sugar

2 tablespoons blackstrap molasses

1¹/₂ cups flour

Pinch of salt

1 teaspoon (heaping) baking soda

1 teaspoon (heaping) cinnamon

1 teaspoon (heaping) ground cloves

1 teaspoon (heaping) ginger

Beat the butter, egg, sugar and molasses in a mixer bowl until smooth. Add the flour, salt and baking soda, mixing well. Sift the cinnamon, cloves and ginger together. Stir into the mixture. Shape into 1-inch balls and place on a greased cookie sheet. Bake at 450 degrees for 10 minutes. Cool on a wire rack.

Yield: 15 to 20 cookies

Irish American Heritage Center

SPRITSKRANSAR *Sweden*
SPRITZ RINGS

1 cup butter, softened

¹/₂ cup sifted confectioners' sugar

1 egg yolk

1 teaspoon almond extract

¹/₃ cup ground blanched almonds

2 cups sifted flour

Cream the butter and confectioners' sugar in a mixer bowl until light and fluffy. Stir in the egg yolk and almond extract. Add the ground almonds and flour gradually, stirring until the dough is smooth and firm. Press through a cookie press fitted with a ring or "S" disk onto a buttered cookie sheet. Bake at 375 degrees for 8 to 10 minutes or until golden. Cool on the cookie sheet.

Yield: 45 cookies

Aina Momquist, Linnea South Suburban Swedish Women's Club

DESSERTS

For Scottish Shortbread, cream 2 cups softened butter, 1 cup sugar, 1 cup cornstarch and 3 cups flour in a large bowl. Mix until the dough forms a ball. Press the dough into an ungreased 9x13-inch baking pan. Pierce the surface several times with a fork; sprinkle with sugar. Place in a cold oven. Bake at 350 degrees for 45 minutes or until golden brown. Cut into squares; cool on a wire rack.

Yield: 36 squares

Nancy Strolle, Thistle & Heather Highland Dancers

DESSERTS

This pastry is a must for the holidays. In The Netherlands bakers form the pastry in different shapes for wreaths that are decorated with red and green sweet dried cherries. It is a very delicate pastry. Henny Bos declares that his mother's homebaked banquet was always the best. He still carries on the tradition with his daughters and daughter-in-law. They set aside a day in November to make the pastry, sharing some with friends and freezing the rest for Christmas celebrations.

———

This rich pastry from Greece is offered to guests with a cup of Greek coffee after the meal.

BANQUET *The Netherlands*
ALMOND-FILLED PASTRY

2	cups margarine or butter
4	cups flour
1	cup cold water
1	(16-ounce) package almond paste, broken up
2	cups sugar
3	eggs, beaten
1	teaspoon lemon extract

Cut the margarine into the flour in a large bowl. Add the water and knead until a smooth dough forms. Chill for 8 to 10 hours. Beat the almond paste, sugar, eggs and lemon extract in a medium bowl. Chill for 8 to 10 hours. Roll the dough into a 4x12-inch rectangle on a lightly floured surface. Spread the almond filling down the center. Roll up from the long end, sealing the ends with water. Place on a nonstick baking sheet. Bake at 425 degrees for 20 minutes or until brown.

Yield: 24 to 36 pastries

Henny Bos, Chicago Museum Committee

BAKLAVA *Greece*
HONEY-FILLED PASTRIES

1	pound walnuts, ground
1	pound pecans, ground
1	cup sugar
1	teaspoon cinnamon
2	cups melted butter
1	pound phyllo dough
4	cups sugar
2	cups water
2	tablespoons (heaping) honey
1	cinnamon stick
	Juice from 1/2 lemon

Combine the walnuts, pecans, 1 cup sugar and cinnamon in a bowl. Brush a 9x12 baking pan with some of the melted butter. Stack 8 sheets of the phyllo dough in the pan, brushing each sheet with butter and cutting the sheets to fit. Sprinkle 1 cup of the nut mixture over the layers. Alternate layers of 3 sheets of phyllo dough and 1 cup of the nut mixture until all ingredients have been used, ending with 8 sheets of phyllo and brushing each sheet of dough with melted butter. Cut through the layers diagonally to form diamond-shapes. Bake at 325 degrees for 1 hour or until brown and crispy. Combine 4 cups sugar, water, honey, cinnamon stick and lemon juice in a saucepan. Bring to a boil. Cook for 20 to 30 minutes, stirring often. Let cool completely. Remove cinnamon stick. Spoon over the hot baked pastries. Let stand overnight before serving.

Yield: 24 to 30 servings

Dina Roiniotis, Peiraikon Hellenic School

DESSERTS

Buccellati Siciliani *Italy*
CHRISTMAS FIG AND NUT COOKIES

1	pound figs, chopped
8	ounces pignoli (pine nuts)
8	ounces red seedless raisins
8	ounces white seedless raisins
8	ounces chopped walnuts
8	ounces chopped almonds
8	ounces chopped pecans
8	ounces freshly grated lemon peel
8	ounces freshly grated orange peel
1	to 2 ounces whiskey
1	teaspoon honey
4	teaspoons cinnamon
1	cup sugar
1	pound lard
1	cup sugar
3	eggs
1	teaspoon vanilla extract
1	cup milk
5	cups sifted flour
1	tablespoon baking powder
1	teaspoon salt

Combine the figs, pignoli, raisins, walnuts, almonds, pecans, lemon and orange peel, whiskey, honey, cinnamon and 1 cup sugar in a medium bowl; mix well. Cover and refrigerate for 24 hours. Cream the lard and 1 cup sugar in a mixer bowl until light and fluffy. Beat the eggs, vanilla, milk, flour, baking powder and salt in a bowl. Add to the creamed mixture, stirring well. Let stand for 4 hours. Roll the dough into 3x8-inch pieces. Cut each piece into four 2-inch long portions. Spoon 1 teaspoon of the fig filling in the center of each, leaving a ¹/₄-inch border. Roll up and shape into crescents. Pierce the ends with a fork or make 3 slices on the curve of the cookie with a knife for decoration. Place on a nonstick cookie sheet. Bake at 350 degrees for 15 to 20 minutes. Cool on a wire rack. May frost and decorate with rainbow candy sprinkles.

Yield: 50 to 60 cookies

Eleonora Fruscione

TO PREPARE CROATIAN PITA, MIX 3 CUPS FLOUR AND 1 TEASPOON BAKING POWDER IN A BOWL. CUT IN 1 CUP SOFTENED BUTTER UNTIL CRUMBLY. ADD 2 BEATEN EGGS AND 1 CUP SUGAR, MIXING WELL. DIVIDE THE DOUGH INTO 2 EQUAL PORTIONS. ROLL EACH PORTION INTO A 10x15-INCH RECTANGLE. LINE A 10x15-INCH BAKING PAN WITH 1 PORTION OF THE DOUGH. TOSS 2 POUNDS THINLY SLICED APPLES WITH ¹/₂ TEASPOON CINNAMON AND 2 TABLESPOONS SUGAR. SPOON EVENLY OVER THE DOUGH. TOP WITH THE REMAINING DOUGH. BAKE AT 350 DEGREES FOR 45 MINUTES. CUT INTO SQUARES TO SERVE.

YIELD: 24 SERVINGS

LILLIAN QUATCHAK, SACRED HEART CROATIAN SCHOOL, KOLO AND TAMBURA GROUP

DESSERTS

To make the Cream Cheese Pastry for the cookies, cream 6 ounces cream cheese and 1 cup softened butter in a mixer bowl until light and fluffy. Sift 2 cups flour and $1/2$ of a 4-ounce package French Vanilla pudding and pie filling mix 5 times. Cut into the creamed mixture with a pastry cutter. Knead until smooth; shape into a ball. Wrap in floured foil and chill until firm.

———

For Walnut Filling for the butter horns, beat 2 egg whites in a bowl until foamy. Add $1/2$ cup sugar, beating until stiff peaks form. Fold in 1 cup finely ground walnuts and $1/2$ teaspoon walnut extract.

ROSZKI *Czech Republic*

CHEESE-FILLED COOKIES

8	ounces cream cheese
1	(4-ounce) package French vanilla pudding and pie filling mix
$1/2$	cup sugar
2	tablespoons cornstarch
	Cream Cheese Pastry (at left)
	Confectioners' sugar

Mix cream cheese, pudding mix, sugar and cornstarch in a double boiler. Cook over boiling water for 20 minutes, stirring frequently. Remove from the heat and let cool. Chill for 1 hour. Roll out the Cream Cheese Pastry to $1/8$-inch thickness. Cut into $1^1/2$-inch squares. Place half of the squares on a 10x17-inch nonstick baking pan. Place 1 teaspoon of the cream cheese filling on each square. Top with the remaining squares, sealing the edges. Bake at 350 degrees for 15 minutes. Cool on a wire rack. Sprinkle with confectioners' sugar.

Yield: 36 cookies

Joseph Straka

Czech Republic

BUTTER HORNS

2	cups sifted flour
1	teaspoon baking powder
$1/4$	teaspoon salt
$1/2$	cup butter or margarine, softened
1	teaspoon (heaping) yeast
2	tablespoons warm water
2	egg yolks, slightly beaten
$1/4$	cup sour cream
$1/2$	teaspoon vanilla extract
	Walnut Filling (at left)

Sift the flour, baking powder and salt into a large bowl. Cut in the butter until the mixture is crumbly. Dissolve the yeast in the warm water in a bowl. Add the egg yolks, sour cream and vanilla, mixing well. Stir into the dry ingredients. Chill for 1 hour. Divide the dough into 4 equal portions. Place on a surface sprinkled with confectioners' sugar. Roll each portion into a 9-inch circle and cut each into 6 wedges. Place 1 teaspoon of the Walnut Filling on each wedge. Roll up from the large end, shaping into crescents. Place on a nonstick baking pan. Bake at 400 degrees for 12 to 15 minutes or until golden brown.

Yield: 24 crescents

Club Bedrich Smetana

A SEASON OF CELEBRATING

Canada
NANAIMO BARS

1/2 cup butter, softened

1/4 cup sugar

5 tablespoons baking cocoa

1 teaspoon vanilla extract

1 egg, beaten

2 cups graham cracker crumbs

1 cup shredded coconut

1/2 cup chopped walnuts

1/4 cup butter, softened

3 tablespoons milk

2 tablespoons vanilla custard powder

2 cups confectioners' sugar

4 ounces semisweet chocolate

1 tablespoon butter

Mix 1/2 cup butter, sugar, cocoa, vanilla and egg in a bowl. Place over another bowl full of hot water. Stir until the butter has melted. Combine the graham cracker crumbs, coconut and walnuts in a small bowl. Stir into the cocoa mixture. Press into a 9-inch square pan. Cream 1/4 cup butter in a mixer bowl until light and fluffy. Add the milk and vanilla custard powder. Stir in the confectioners' sugar. Spread over the cocoa mixture. Chill for 15 minutes. Melt the semisweet chocolate and 1 tablespoon butter in a double boiler over hot water, stirring until smooth. Spread evenly over the chilled layers. Chill until firm; remove from refrigerator several minutes before serving. Cut into squares.

Yield: 12 servings
The Canadian Women's Club of Chicago

A VERSION OF THESE NO-BAKE BARS DEVELOPED IN THE CANADIAN KITCHENS OF A WELL KNOWN FOOD COMPANY WAS CHRISTENED "NANAIMO BARS" AFTER THE CITY OF THAT NAME ON VANCOUVER ISLAND. NANAIMO (FROM SNENY-MO, A LOCAL INDIAN TERM FOR A LOOSE CONFEDERATION OF FIVE BANDS) STARTED AS A HUDSON BAY TRADING POST IN 1849.

Italy
CRISPELLES

4 cups flour

1 1/2 teaspoons baking powder

8 eggs, beaten

1 teaspoon vanilla extract

Anisette extract

Oil for frying

Honey and confectioners' sugar

Mix the flour and baking powder in a bowl. Add the eggs and vanilla. Knead until a soft dough forms. Roll out thinly. Cut into 4- to 5-inch long strips. Make a slit in the center of the strips and pull one end of the strip through the opening to form a bow. Drop the bows into hot oil in a skillet. Fry just until golden brown; drain on paper towels. Drizzle with honey and sprinkle with confectioners' sugar.

Yield: 4 dozen crispelles
Marie Palello, Joint Civic Committee of Italian Americans

MARIE PALELLO'S MOTHER, JOSEPHINE DALLESANDRO BROUGHT THIS RECIPE FOR CRISPELLES FROM HER NATIVE SACRONI, ITALY, IN 1928. SHE ONLY MADE THESE COOKIES AT CHRISTMAS TIME WITH THE HELP OF HER HUSBAND, AND LATER A FRIEND. MARIE ASKED HER MOTHER TO SHOW HER HOW TO MAKE THE CRISPELLES SINCE SHE FEARED THAT WHEN HER MOTHER WAS GONE, THE TRADITION WOULD BE LOST FOR THE NEXT GENERATION. NOW SHE MAKES THEM FOR HER FAMILY, WHO ENJOY THEM EVERY CHRISTMAS, AND TELL HER THAT "THEY REALLY TASTE LIKE GRANDMA MADE THEM."

DESSERTS

Shalini D'Souza fondly recalls preparing kulkuls with her mother and sisters at Christmas time. They sang carols, told jokes and talked, and competed to see who could prepare the most kulkuls and whose did not open up when fried. These crunchy delicacies are served after midnight mass and throughout the Christmas season to family and friends.

Khrystyky *Belarus*

CRULLERS

The brandy added to this mixture prevents the crullers from absorbing too much oil during frying. They are very fragile, so handle with care!

4	egg yolks, beaten
2	tablespoons sugar
2	tablespoons sour cream
1	tablespoon brandy
1¹/₂	cups flour
¹/₂	teaspoon salt
	Oil for frying
	Confectioners' sugar

Beat the egg yolks and sugar in a bowl until frothy. Stir in the sour cream, brandy, flour and salt. Knead on a lightly floured surface until a soft dough forms. Roll out thinly. Cut into 1-inch-wide strips, then cut diagonally to form diamond shapes. Cut a slit in the center of each diamond. Pull the two points through the slit to form the khrystyky. Fry in hot oil in a skillet just until light brown. Drain on paper towels; cool slightly. Sprinkle with confectioners' sugar. Store in an airtight container.

Yield: 25 to 35 khrystyky

Raisa Bratkiv, Bielarusian Coordinating Committee of Chicago

Kulkuls *India*

FRIED CHRISTMAS COOKIES

10	cups maida or all-purpose flour
1¹/₂	teaspoons baking powder
3	tablespoons butter, softened
	Sugar and salt to taste
	Liquid from 1¹/₂ coconuts
	Oil for frying
3	to 5 cups sugar
1	cup water

Sift the maida and baking powder into a bowl. Cut in the butter. Mix some sugar and salt to taste with a small amount of the coconut liquid and pour into the mixture. Knead until a soft dough forms, adding more coconut liquid for desired consistency. Let stand, covered, for 10 to 15 minutes. Shape dough into 1-inch balls. Flatten with fork, rolling backwards firmly to leave the marks of the fork on the outside. Drop into hot oil in a deep skillet. Fry until golden brown. Remove with slotted spoon; drain overnight. Heat 3 cups sugar in water in a saucepan until a thick syrup forms, adding more sugar as needed. Drop in the kulkuls, turning to coat. Cool on waxed paper to prevent sticking.

Yield: 15 servings

Shalini D'Souza, India Catholic Association of America

DESSERTS

LISTY *Czech Republic*

FRIED PASTRY LEAVES

¹/₂   cup flour

Dash of salt

1   teaspoon confectioners' sugar

3   egg yolks, beaten

1¹/₂ tablespoons cream

1   tablespoon whiskey

Oil for frying

Confectioners' sugar

Combine the flour, salt and 1 teaspoon confectioners' sugar in a bowl. Add the egg yolks, cream and whiskey, beating well. Knead on a floured surface until the dough is no longer sticky. Roll out thinly. Cut into 1x2-inch pieces. Cut a slit in the center. Fry 3 at a time in hot oil in a heavy skillet until light brown, being careful not to burn. Turn only once. Drain on paper towels; cool. Sprinkle with confectioners' sugar.

Yield: 12 servings

Club Bedrich Smetana

NAORIES *India*

FRIED FILLED PASTRIES

2   ounces walnuts, crushed

2   ounces pistachios, chopped

4   ounces raisins, finely chopped

2   tablespoons Kus Kus (poppy seeds)

1¹/₂ cups shredded dried coconut

1   cup sugar

6   cups flour

¹/₂   teaspoon salt

¹/₄   cup butter

Milk

Oil for deep-frying

Combine the walnuts, pistachios, raisins, Kus Kus, coconut and sugar in a saucepan. Simmer over low heat for 10 minutes, stirring constantly. Remove from the heat. Combine the flour and salt in a bowl. Cut in the butter. Add enough milk to form a soft dough. Roll ¹/₈ inch thick on a lightly floured surface. Cut into 3-inch circles. Place 1 teaspoon of the nut filling on one half of the circle. Fold over, sealing the edge with milk and crimping with a fork. Drop into hot oil in a deep fryer. Fry until golden brown. Drain well and let cool. Store in an airtight container.

Yield: 4 dozen pastries

Dottie D'Souza, India Catholic Association of America

Desserts

Italians celebrate St. Lucia's Day, which honors the patron saint of light and is observed with blazing bonfires and torchlight processions.

CHRUŚCIK *Poland*

POLISH BOWS

6 egg yolks

2 tablespoons sugar

2 cups flour

$^1/_2$ teaspoon salt

$^1/_2$ cup sour cream

1 teaspoon vanilla extract

1 teaspoon grated lemon peel

$^1/_4$ cup rum

Oil for frying

Beat the egg yolks in a bowl until thick and lemon-colored. Add the sugar gradually, beating well. Fold in the flour and salt alternately with the sour cream. Stir in the vanilla, lemon peel and rum. Knead for 15 minutes on a floured surface. Separate into 4 equal portions. Roll out thinly, loosening the dough from the surface and turning often. Cut into $1^1/_2$x4-inch strips. Cut a slit near one end of each strip; bring the other end through the opening to form a bow. Heat the oil to 375 degrees in a deep fryer. Fry quickly until light brown. Drain on paper towels. Dust with confectioners' sugar.

Yield: 24 to 36 bows

Joan Pitchford, Lansing Business Women's Association

ST. JOSEPH'S DAY SFINGI *Italy*

ITALIAN PUFFED DOUGHNUTS

16 ounces ricotta cheese

$^1/_2$ cup sugar

6 eggs, beaten

1 tablespoon vanilla extract

$2^1/_2$ cups self-rising flour

Oil for frying

Combine the ricotta cheese, sugar, eggs and vanilla in a bowl and mix well. Add the flour and mix until well blended. Dough should be the consistency of thick pancake batter. Heat the oil to 350 degrees in a deep fryer. Drop the batter by heaping tablespoonfuls into the hot oil. Fry for 4 to 8 minutes or until golden brown. Remove with a slotted spoon; drain on paper towels. Dust with confectioners' sugar if desired.

Yield: 4 dozen

Mary Scalera, Villa Scalabrini Home for the Aged

FUESENT OR NONNE FASTEN *Luxembourg*
LUXEMBOURG DOUGHNUTS

1 envelope dry yeast

1/2 cup warm milk

1 teaspoon sugar

3 1/2 cups plus
2 tablespoons flour

4 eggs, at room
temperature

1 teaspoon salt

1/2 cup sugar

1/2 cup melted butter,
cooled to lukewarm

Vegetable oil for
deep-frying

Dissolve yeast in warm milk with 1 teaspoon sugar in a large bowl. Sprinkle with 2 table-spoons of the flour. Let stand, covered, for 15 minutes. Stir 1/2 cup of the flour into the yeast mixture. Add the eggs, salt and 1/2 cup sugar, mixing well. Stir in 1/2 cup of the flour. Stir in the butter. Add enough of the remaining flour to make a soft dough. Knead well. Let stand, covered, for 15 minutes. Turn out onto a floured surface. Roll out to a 1/2-inch thickness. Cut into 3-inch circles. Cut leftover dough into strips and tie into knots. Place on floured baking sheets. Let stand, covered, until doubled in bulk. Deep-fry in medium-hot oil until golden brown, turning once. Drain on paper towels. Roll in a mixture of sugar and cinnamon or dust with confectioners' sugar.

Yield: 2 to 3 dozen
Madeleine Thomé

OLIEBOLLEN *The Netherlands*
DUTCH DOUGHNUTS

3 eggs, beaten

4 teaspoons baking
powder

4 cups flour

1 1/2 cups sugar

2 large apples, chopped

2/3 cup raisins

2 cups milk

1 teaspoon vanilla
extract

Pinch of salt

Oil for deep-frying

Combine the eggs, baking powder, flour and sugar in a large bowl; mix well. Stir in the apples, raisins, milk, vanilla and salt. Drop by tablespoonfuls into hot oil in a deep fryer. Deep-fry until golden brown. Remove with a slotted spoon and drain on paper towels. Sprinkle with confectioners' sugar before serving. Serve warm.

Yield: 4 dozen
Cindy Sluis, Chicago Museum Committee

DESSERTS

MADELEINE THOMÉ'S GRANDFATHER SAYS THAT PEOPLE IN LUXEMBOURG EAT LOTS OF THESE DOUGHNUTS BEFORE LENT TO FATTEN UP BEFORE THE FASTING PERIOD BETWEEN ASH WEDNESDAY AND EASTER SUNDAY. PEOPLE SAY "MIR MACHEN FUESEND," BUT THE DOUGHNUTS ARE ALSO CALLED "NONNE FASTEN."

———

OLIEBOLLEN ARE THE ANCESTORS OF THE AMERICAN DOUGHNUT, WHICH THE PILGRIMS LEARNED TO MAKE FROM THEIR DUTCH NEIGHBORS IN AMSTERDAM BEFORE SAILING TO THE NEW WORLD. THE DUTCH HAVE A TRADITION OF MAKING OLIEBOLLEN FOR NEW YEAR'S EVE AND MANY FAMILIES ARE BUSY MAKING THEM ON THE LAST DAY OF THE YEAR. SOME FAMILIES KEPT THIS TRADITION WHEN THEY EMIGRATED TO THE UNITED STATES.

LIST OF CONTRIBUTORS

Karen Aagaard

Anna-Maria Adair

A Friend of The Museum of Science and Industry

Rose Aranha, India Catholic Association of America

Maria T. Arellano, Chicago Ecuadorean Lions Club

Carol Bach, Danish Sisterhood Society, Olga Lodge 11

Yelva Baelum, Danish American Athletic Club

Maria Bappert, Society of the Danube Swabians

Carol Bart

Ximena Bastidas, Chicago Ecuadorean Lions Club

Gail Bergren, Lansing Business Women's Association

Renee Berian, Armenian Youth Federation

Mary Bonicky, Sacred Heart Croatian School, Kolo and Tambura Group

Henny Bos, Chicago Museum Committee

Olga Bradley, Belizean Cultural Association

Raisa Bratkiv, Bielarusian Coordinating Committee of Chicago

Anna Bruszkiewicz, Bielarusian Coordinating Committee of Chicago

Calvin Reformed Church of Lynwood, Illinois

The Canadian Women's Club of Chicago

Tom Carvalho, India Catholic Association of America

Elsie Castellino, India Catholic Association of America

Ginger Cheung, Chinese American Civic Council

Liang Chiung-pai

Club Bedrich Smetana

Angela Cole

Jaclen Cole, Linnea South Suburban Swedish Women's Club

Gloria Comstock, Linnea South Suburban Swedish Women's Club

Consulate General of Guatemala

Consulate General of Israel to the Midwest

Josephine Crame, Sacred Heart Croatian School, Kolo and Tambura Group

Mary Cromey, Society of the Danube Swabians

Anna Diestl, Society of the Danube Swabians

Katharina Diestl, Society of the Danube Swabians

Ulla Dimmick, Linnea South Suburban Swedish Women's Club

Mary and Tony Dinolfo

Dottie D'Souza, India Catholic Association of America

Netta D'Souza, India Catholic Association of America

Shalini D'Souza, India Catholic Association of America

Susan D'Souza, India Catholic Association of America

Helga Edman, Linnea South Suburban Swedish Women's Club

Embassy of Israel

Isabella Erbe, Society of the Danube Swabians

Pam Ferreira, India Catholic Association of America

Joey Filingeri

Eleonora Fruscione

Helen Gabourel, Belizean Cultural Association

Helen Gall, Calvin Reformed Church of Lynwood, Illinois

Vonda Gluck (Chippewa), Native American Tree Committee

Laurie Grant, Thistle & Heather Highland Dancers

Mary Griffin, Irish American Heritage Center

Birdy Haggerty-Francis, Belizean Cultural Association

Virginia Hast, Linnea South Suburban Swedish Women's Club

Anni Hoffmann, Society of the Danube Swabians

Irish American Heritage Center

Lucy Jalamov, Bielarusian Coordinating Committee of Chicago

Alice Jung

Barbara Kaffka, Calvin Reformed Church of Lynwood, Illinois

Eeva Kallio, Finnladies of Chicagoland

Loliya Kantarovich, Bielarusian Coordinating Committee of Chicago

Bernice Kasarski

Mary N. Khair, St. Mark's Coptic Church

Alberta Kontos, Lansing Business Women's Association

Maria Kreiling, Society of the Danube Swabians

Anita Kropp

Marta Kuczura, Bielarusian Coordinating Committee of Chicago

Elizabeth Kulas, Bielarusian Coordinating Committee of Chicago

Margaret Kun, Calvin Reformed Church of Lynwood, Illinois

Judy Kupfer

Toni Laakso, Finnladies of Chicagoland

Sofia Latuszkin, Belarusian American National Council of Chicago

Lorraine Leider, Linnea South Suburban Swedish Women's Club

Pat LeNoble, Thistle & Heather Highland Dancers

Adrianna Liakos, Peiraikon Hellenic School

Sophie Liambotis, Peiraikon Hellenic School

Anna Livaditis, Peiraikon Hellenic School

Donna Lively, Lansing Business Women's Association

Gertrude Lobo, India Catholic Association of America

Mrs. A. MacFarlane, Belizean Cultural Association

Anna Maieritsch, Society of the Danube Swabians

Jacintha B. Martis, India Catholic Association of America

Rosa Mata, Chicago Ecuadorean Lions Club

Mary Ellen McNicholas, Irish American Heritage Center

Evelyn Devivo Meine

Lucy Menezes, India Catholic Association of America

Rosemary Mittenthal, Sampaguita Singers of Chicago, Inc.

Aina Momquist, Linnea South Suburban Swedish Women's Club

Nora Murphy, Irish American
Heritage Center
Alice Nakashima
Christina Newenhouse, Finnladies of
Chicagoland
Zoya Nikiforovich, Bielarusian
Coordinating Committee of Chicago
Theresa Ochoa, Chicago Mexica
Lions Club
Roy Okamoto
Marie Palello, Joint Civic Committee of
Italian Americans
Pat Paprocki, India Catholic Association
of America
Eva Pfaff, Society of the Danube Swabians
Joan Pitchford, Lansing Business Women's
Association
Polish Scouting Organization,
Z.H.P.—Inc.
Erma Prewett, Danish Sisterhood Society,
Olga Lodge 177
Elizabeth Putz, Society of the
Danube Swabians
Lillian Quatchak, Sacred Heart Croatian
School, Kolo and Tambura Group
Mariette Rao, India Catholic Association
of America
Anni Ratschan, Society of the
Danube Swabians
Lydia Ringus, Knights of Lithuanian
Dancers
Eva Ritter, Society of the
Danube Swabians
Dina Roiniotis, Peiraikon Hellenic School
The Romanian Christmas Group
Holy Nativity
Vera Romuk, Bielarusian Coordinating
Committee of Chicago
Margie Rysner, Chicago Museum
Committee
Mary Scalera, Villa Scalabrini Home for
the Aged
Kathérina Scheero, Society of the Danube
Swabians

Gladys Schneider, Linnea South Suburban
Swedish Women's Club
Marianne B. Schroeder, Society of the
Danube Swabians
Hilde Sendef, Society of the
Danube Swabians
Eula Sequeira, India Catholic Association
of America
Kay Shevlin, Irish American
Heritage Center
Joanne Sideris, Peiraikon Hellenic School
Joyce Simunovic, Sacred Heart Croatian
School, Kolo and Tambura Committee
Ann Simunovic-Goetz, Sacred Heart
Croatian School, Kolo and
Tambura Group
Sharon Skolnick (Apache), Native
American Tree Committee
Cindy Sluis, The Chicago Museum
Committee
Jean Smoots, Linnea South Suburban
Swedish Women's Club
Society of the Danube Swabians
Anna Stengel, Society of the
Danube Swabians
Joseph Straka
Nancy Strolle, Thistle & Heather
Highland Dancers
Jean Svedberg, Linnea South Suburban
Swedish Women's Club
Birgit Swanson, Linnea South Suburban
Swedish Women's Club
Swiss Club of Chicago
Tampopo-Kai
Emma Tezak, Sacred Heart Croatian
School, Kolo and Tambura Group
Rosemary Thalanany, India Catholic
Association of America
Madeleine Thomé
Enell Thurston, Belizean Cultural
Association
Mary Tomacic, Croatian Women's
Organization, Branch 1,
Chicago, Illinois

Gordana Trbuhovich, Federation of
Circles of Serbian Sisters, Midwestern
Metropolitanate of the Serbian
Orthodox Church
Miryana Trbuhovich, Federation of Circles
of Serbian Sisters, Midwestern
Metropolitanate of the Serbian
Orthodox Church
Margaret V. Tredon, Danish Sisterhood
Society, Olga Lodge 11
Lynette "Lineaka" Troha, Stars of the
South Pacific
Rosalie Turner, Linnea South Suburban
Swedish Women's Club
Ukrainian National Women's League,
Branch 22, in Chicago
Vala Vakselis, Bielarusian Coordinating
Committee of Chicago
Barb VeSota
Lucille VeSota
Dwight O. Von Ahnen, German-
American Children's Chorus
Beatrice Weiss, Swiss Club of Chicago
Lillian Wennlund, Linnea South Suburban
Swedish Women's Club
Riitta M. West
Jean Weyrich
Ann Williams, Cambrian Benevolent
Society of Chicago
Ellenor Williams, Cambrian Benevolent
Society of Chicago
Elizabeth Wolf, Society of the
Danube Swabians
Julia Brown Wolf, Lakota (Sioux), Native
American Tree Committee
Alycia Wright
Taye Yamaguchi
Rabbi Ira S. Youdovin, Chicago Board
of Rabbis

INDEX BY COUNTRY

INDEX BY CATEGORY

A SEASON OF CELEBRATING

To order additional copies of

A Season of Celebrating

mail your order to:

The Museum Shops
Museum of Science and Industry
57th Street and Lake Shore Drive
Chicago, Illinois 60637

or

fax your order to:
(773) 684-8853
or phone:
(773) 684-1414, Ext. 2476
or visit our webstite: http://www.msichicago.org

When ordering, please provide the following information:

Name, Museum Member Number (for 10% discount), Address,
Zip Code, and Telephone Number

Indicate the Method of Payment:

(Visa, MC, Discover, Amex, Diner or Check or Money Order)

If ordering by mail or fax and paying by credit card indicate:

Credit Card Number, Expiration Date, and Signature

The cost per book is:

$18.95 less 10% Museum Member Discount if applicable
(Illinois residents please add 8.75% sales tax)
and include appropriate Shipping and Handling amount
according to the chart below:

Shipping and Handling:	
$10.01 to $25.00	$4.50
$25.01 to $40.00	$6.50
$40.01 to $55.00	$7.95
$55.01 to $75.00	$8.50
$75.01 to $100.00	$9.95
$100.00+	$11.50